DIAMOND BOOKS

The **blue section** answers the question 'I would like to see or do something; where do I go and what do I see when I get there?' This section is arranged as an alphabetical list of topics. It is recommended that an up-to-date atlas or street plan is used in conjunction with the location maps in this section. Within each topic you will find:

- A selection of the best examples on offer.
- How to get there, costs and opening times for each entry.
- The outstanding features of each entry.
- A simplified map, with each entry plotted and the nearest landmark or transport access.

The **red section** is a lively and informative gazetteer. It offers:
- Essential facts about the main places and cultural items.
  What is La Bastille? Who was Michelangelo? Where is Delphi?

The **gold section** is full of practical and invaluable travel information. It offers:
- Everything you need to know to help you enjoy yourself and get the most out of your time away, from Accommodation through Baby-sitters, Car Hire, Food, Health, Money, Newspapers, Taxis and Telephones to Youth Hostels.

1993 PRICES	Inexpensive	Moderate	Expensive
Attractions Ancient Rome, Museums, etc.	under L.6000	L.6000-L.10,000	over L.10,000
Restaurants Main course	under L.15,000	L.15,000-L.25,000	over L.25,000
Nightlife Drinks		under L.10,000	over L.10,000

Cross-references:

Type in small capitals – CHURCHES – tells you that more information on an item is available within the topic on churches.

A-Z after an item tells you that more information is available within the gazetteer. Simply look under the appropriate name.

A name in bold – **Holy Cathedral** – also tells you that more information on an item is available in the gazetteer – again simply look up the name.

CONTENTS

CONTENTS

Colosseo

INTRODUCTION

A visit to Rome is one of life's great experiences. It is a city of extraordinary contrasts: between the ancient and the modern, and between the sacred and the profane. It is an exhilarating place but equally it can be exasperating: ancient ruins which once echoed to the footsteps of Julius Caesar and Augustus are assaulted by the noise and pollution of the city traffic only metres away; pilgrims from every nation crowd St. Peter's Square (Piazza San Pietro) in homage to the seat of Christendom, while newsstands on every street corner display acres of pornographic magazines and videos. Such contrasts, however, perhaps only serve to illustrate that Rome really *is* the Eternal City. It has survived many invasions, wars and political and religious upheavals over the centuries and no doubt it will also triumph over contemporary evils.

The rise of Rome from its humble origins to become the *caput mondi* – 'capital of the world' – whose laws, technology, culture and religion spread throughout the known world, is a story of enduring fascination. According to legend, Rome was founded by Romulus and Remus, whose mother was Rhea Silvia, a vestal virgin, and father Mars, the god of war. The infant twins were abandoned on the Palatine Hill, where they were suckled by a she-wolf. When they grew up they began building a new city, but in an argument about what to call it, Romulus slew his brother and called it Roma after himself. Archaeological evidence, on the other hand, suggests that the city began as a small farming community on the Palatine at least a century before its supposed foundation by Romulus in 753 BC. The collaboration of this pastoral community with other tribes sparked the growth of the city under the Sabine and then Etruscan kings, and the city gradually spread over the the rest of the Seven Hills of Rome: the Aventine (Aventino), Capitol or Capitoline (Campidoglio), Esquiline (Esquilino), Quirinal (Quirinale), Viminal (Viminale) and Caelian (Celio) hills. After the founding of the Republic in 509 BC, a series of defensive wars evolved into aggressive campaigns of expansion, including the defeat of Carthage (146 BC) and Caesar's expeditions against Gaul and Britain (58-53 BC), until under Trajan the Roman Empire reached its greatest extent, bestraddling the ancient world from the Atlantic to the Black Sea. Recurrent political instability and economic decay, combined with external attacks by barbarian

Ponte Fibracio, Isola Tiberina

tribes, gradually weakened the empire, divided into East and West by Diocletian in AD 286, until in 476 the last emperor, Romulus Augustulus, was deposed by the German Odoacer. Thereafter, European princes, aristocratic Italian families and the papacy struggled for possession of the city, while its population dwindled from one million at the height of the empire to 20,000 in the 12thC. However, many of Rome's most beautiful churches date from these dark centuries.

In 1308 Pope Clement V transferred the papal residence to Avignon, and through the ensuing decades of the French exile and then the Great Schism, the city fell into a pitiable state, its crumbling monuments surrounded by filth and squalor. It was not until the return of Pope Martin V in 1420 that the city began to revive and interest in the classical age began to resurface, and under the pontificates of Julius II and Leo X the city emerged as a centre of Renaissance art and culture.

The brutal Sack of Rome by German and Spanish troops in 1527 blunted Renaissance optimism, but the city survived and, fuelled by the Counter-Reformation in the 16th and 17thC, witnessed the splendours of the Baroque embodied in the construction of new churches, palaces, fountains and streets under the presiding genius of Bernini.

In the 19thC the Risorgimento led by Garibaldi and Mazzini eventually

united Italy under the House of Savoy, confining the political power of the papacy to the Vatican, and in 1870 Rome was declared the capital of the new nation. At that time the walls of the Jewish Ghetto were finally torn down and Jews were given the same rights as other citizens. In the 20thC the city has survived Fascism and Mussolini's dictatorship, and mercifully escaped serious bombardment in World War II.

The result of such a long and eventful history is that modern Rome is quite literally a city built on the layers of the past. Thus, in many cases, a visit to a church, for example San Clemente, Santa Cecilia in Trastevere or Sant'Agnese fuori le Mura, turns out to be a fascinating exploration of earlier buildings underneath as well.

Rome's attractions are so numerous that, during a brief stay, it would

San Pietro in Vaticano

be impossible to explore every ruin, visit every church and museum, and get to know all the streets. There are, however, certain priorities. At the heart of the ancient city are the Palatine and Forum, filled with ruined temples, palaces and civic buildings in which figures such as Caesar and Antony, Augustus and Livia and their imperial successors once worshipped, entertained and governed; unmissable too are the Colosseo, scene of spectacular and savage entertainments, and the Pantheon, a masterpiece of Roman architecture. Despite reconstruction, churches such as Santa Maria Maggiore, with its magnificent gilded coffered ceiling, or Santa Prassede, containing exquisite 9thC mosaics, retain the imprint of their early Christian origins. Evocative of the medieval city are the simple Romanesque church of Santa Maria in Cosmedin, and the narrow streets of the old quarter around Piazza Campo dei Fiori. Dating from the Renaissance are the Palazzo Farnese, the finest of Rome's many impressive palaces, Piazza del Campidoglio, Michelangelo's architectural triumph on the Capitol Hill, and his *Pietà*, a sculpture of breathtaking pathos in St. Peter's. From the Baroque age, whose monuments can be found all over the city, are Bernini's delightful fountains, his magnificent contributions to the interior of St. Peter's, and, outside the basilica, his famous colonnaded piazza. No visit to the city can be complete without a visit to the Vatican Museums (Musei Vaticani), which house the world's most valuable treasures from every age, including the famous classical sculptures of *Apollo Belvedere* and the *Laocoön*, Raphael's frescoed *Stanze*, and Michelangelo's ceiling and *Last Judgment* in the Sistine Chapel (Cappella Sistina).

There are of course some less pleasant aspects of the city that the visitor should be aware of. The traffic has already been touched on – crossing the road can initially seem like an unequal gladiatorial combat between flesh and machine! You will, however, discover that Roman drivers do stop for pedestrians (or swerve round them) once they have stepped onto the road. Beware of pickpockets and bag-snatchers, particularly on public transport, and of groups of Gypsy children who may appear to be begging but who often try to rob unsuspecting tourists. Be sure to check prices before sitting down at cafés, as many charge exorbitant sums for the privilege compared with standing at the bar. Finally, be prepared for at least one of the major tourist attractions to be undergoing restoration, shrouded from view by scaffolding and green netting. These minor irritants aside, Rome has so much to offer: as well as its historic and artistic treasures, there are the wonderful (if unaffordable) shops around Piazza di Spagna, delicious food and drink, and, above all, the exuberant and lively atmosphere of the Eternal City.

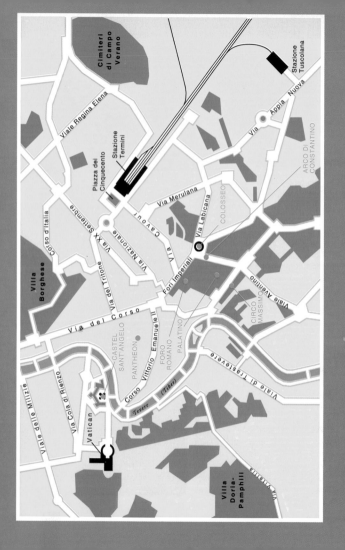

COLOSSEO Colosseum, Piazza del Colosseo.
■ 0900-1800 Mon., Tue. & Thu.-Sat., 0900-1300 Wed. & Sun.
Ⓜ Colosseo. ● Moderate.
Famous site of ancient Rome's gory contests. See **A-Z**.

FORO ROMANO Roman Forum, Via dei Fori Imperiali.
■ 0900-1600 (last admission) Mon. & Wed.-Sat., 0900-1200 (last admission) Sun. Ⓜ Colosseo. ● Expensive (includes admission to the Palatino). *The focal point of life in ancient Rome. See* **A-Z**.

PALATINO Palatine Hill, Via di San Gregorio.
■ Same times and prices as for Foro Romano. Ⓜ Colosseo.
The cradle of Rome, where legend has it that a she-wolf nursed infants Romulus and Remus, and the site of luxurious imperial villas. See **A-Z**.

ARCO DI CONSTANTINO Arch of Constantine, Piazza del Colosseo. Ⓜ Colosseo.
Triumphal arch built in AD 315 to commemorate Emperor Constantine's (see **A-Z***) victory over Maxentius at the Milvian Bridge. See* **A-Z**.

CIRCO MASSIMO Circus Maximus, Via del Circo Massimo.
Ⓜ Circo Massimo.
Vast stadium which, from the 4thC BC, was the site of chariot races and athletics contests. See **A-Z**.

PANTHEON Piazza della Rotonda.
■ 0900-1300. Bus 87, 94. ● Free.
Dating from the 2ndC AD, this magnificent domed temple (now a church) is an architectural wonder of the ancient world. See **A-Z**.

CASTEL SANT'ANGELO Lungotevere Castello.
■ 0900-1300 Tue., Wed., Fri. & Sat., 1400-1800 Mon., 0900-1800 Thu., 0900-1200 Sun. Bus 64, 280. ● Moderate.
Originally the mausoleum of Emperor Hadrian (see **A-Z***), this famous monument has also been a fortress, a prison and a papal palace, and is now a museum with military and art collections. See* **MUSEUMS 2**, **A-Z**.

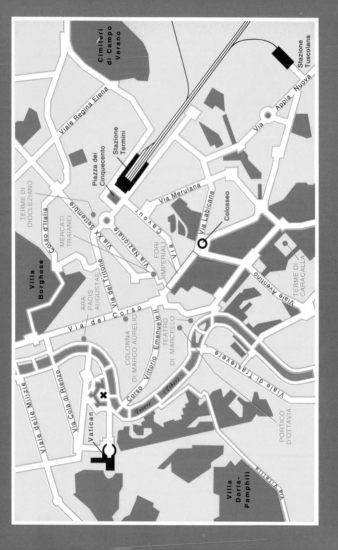

ARA PACIS AUGUSTAE Altar of the Augustan Peace, Via di Ripetta. ■ 0900-1330 Tue.-Sat., also 1600-1900 Tue. & Thu., 0900-1300 Sun. (summer), 0900-1330 Tue.-Sat., 0900-1300 Sun. (winter). Ⓜ Spagna. ● Inexpensive. *Beautiful white marble altar erected in 13 BC after Emperor Augustus' (see **A-Z**) victory over Gaul and Spain. See **A-Z**.*

FORI IMPERIALI Imperial Forums, Via dei Fori Imperiali. Ⓜ Colosseo. *The excavated site includes the forums of Trajan and Augustus (see **A-Z**). See **A-Z**.*

MERCATI TRAIANEI Trajan's Markets, Via IV Novembre 94. ■ 0900-1330 Tue.-Sat., also 1600-1900 Tue. & Thu., 0900-1300 Sun. (summer), 0900-1330 Tue.-Sat., 0900-1300 Sun. & Mon. (winter). Ⓜ Colosseo. ● Inexpensive. *2ndC AD market designed by Apollodorus of Damascus. See **Fori Imperiali**.*

TERME DI DIOCLEZIANO Baths of Diocletian, Piazza della Repubblica. Ⓜ Repubblica. *Site of the largest thermal baths in the Roman Empire (AD 300). See **A-Z**.*

COLONNA DI MARCO AURELIO Colonnade of Marcus Aurelius, Piazza Colonna. Ⓜ Spagna, Barberini. *Erected AD 180-96 to celebrate the victories of Marcus Aurelius. See **A-Z**.*

TEATRO DI MARCELLO Theatre of Marcellus, Via del Teatro di Marcello. Bus 57, 90, 116. *Amphitheatre begun by Julius Caesar and completed by Augustus in 11 BC. Now part of Palazzo Orsini. See **A-Z**.*

TERME DI CARACALLA Baths of Caracalla, Via delle Terme di Caracalla. ■ 0900-1800 Tue.-Sat., 0900-1300 Sun. & Mon. (summer), 0900-1500 Tue.-Sat., 0900-1300 Sun. & Mon. (winter). Ⓜ Circo Massimo. ● Moderate. *These were the most luxurious baths in ancient Rome. See **A-Z**.*

PORTICO D'OTTAVIA Portico of Ottavia, Via del Portico d'Ottavia. Bus 23, 90. *A portico dedicated by Augustus to his sister.*

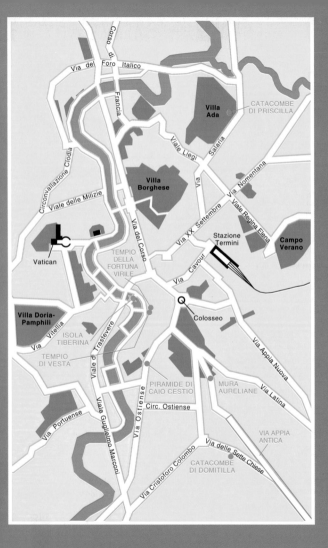

ISOLA TIBERINA Tiber Island, Ponte Fabricio and Ponte Cestio. Bus 23, 26.
Site of the Temple of Aesculapius, god of medicine. See **A-Z**.

MURA AURELIANE Aurelian Wall, Via di Porta San Sebastiano 18.
■ Museo delle Mura 0900-1330 Tue.-Sat. (also 1600-1900 Tue., Thu. & Sat.), 0900-1300 Sun. Bus 118 from the Colosseo. ● Inexpensive.
Massive city wall completed by Emperor Aurelian in AD 279. See **A-Z**.

VIA APPIA ANTICA Appian Way, begins at Porta San Sebastiano. Bus 118 from the Colosseo.
This famous Roman road, which linked the city with Brindisi, is lined with the remains of magnificent monuments and tombs. See **A-Z**.

TEMPIO DELLA FORTUNA VIRILE Temple of Fortuna Virile, Piazza della Bocca della Verità. Bus 90, 92, 94, 95.
Elegant 2ndC BC Republican temple.

TEMPIO DI VESTA Temple of Vesta, Piazza della Bocca della Verità. Bus 90, 92, 94, 95.
Beautiful circular temple dating from the 2ndC BC.

PIRAMIDE DI CAIO CESTIO Pyramid of Caius Cestius, Piazzale Ostiense. Ⓜ Piramide.
The unusual white marble tomb of Caius Cestius, praetor and tribune, who died in 12 BC. See **A-Z**.

CATACOMBE DI DOMITILLA Catacombs of Domitilla, Via delle Sette Chiese 283. ■ 0830-1200, 1430-1730 Wed.-Mon. Bus 218 from San Giovanni in Laterano. ● Moderate.
The largest catacombs in Rome. See **A-Z**.

CATACOMBE DI PRISCILLA Catacombs of Priscilla, Via Salaria 430. ■ 0830-1200, 1430-1730 (1700 in winter) Tue.-Sun. Bus 56 from Piazza Barberini or Bus 57 from Stazione Termini. ● Moderate.
Contain oldest-known painting of the Virgin and Child (2ndC). See **A-Z**.

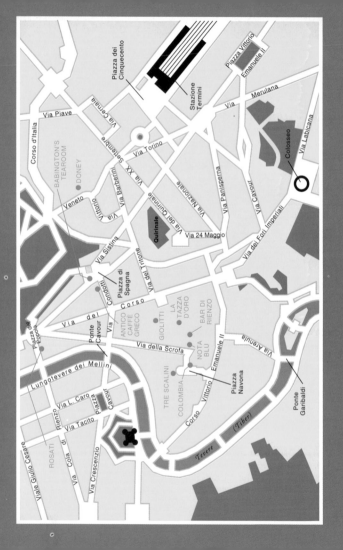

CAFÉS

ANTICO CAFFÈ GRECO Via Condotti 86. ■ 0800-2100 Mon.-Sat.
Ⓜ Spagna. *The décor dates from 1860, when this café was a favourite
haunt of writers, artists and musicians.*

DONEY Via Vittorio Veneto 145. ■ 0800-1300, 1600-2000 Tue.-Sun.
Ⓜ Barberini, Spagna. *A fashionable pavement café on the famous Via
Vittorio Veneto.*

COLOMBIA Piazza Navona 88. ■ 0700-0130 Tue.-Sun. Bus 26, 81.
Relax in the beautiful Piazza Navona (see **A-Z***) over a cup of fine coffee.*

ROSATI Piazza del Popolo 4. ■ 0800-0100 Wed.-Mon. Ⓜ Flaminio.
Offers excellent cocktails, and a wide choice of pastries and cakes.

BABINGTON'S TEAROOM Piazza di Spagna 23. ■ 0900-2030
Fri.-Wed. Ⓜ Spagna. *Favourite (but pricey) meeting place to take tea
English style.*

BAR DI RIENZO Piazza della Rotonda 9. ■ 0730-0230 Wed.-Mon.
Bus 26, 81. *Offers the choice of a full English breakfast or the traditional
cappuccino.*

LA TAZZA D'ORO Via degli Orfani 86. ■ 0700-2200 Mon.-Sat.
Bus 26, 81. *Try some of the best coffee in Rome:* risetto *is strong,* freddo
is iced.

Ice-cream parlours:

GIOLITTI Via degli Uffici del Vicario 40. ■ 0700-0200 Tue.-Sun. Bus
26, 81. *Recognized for 30 years as the king of Rome's ice-cream makers.*

TRE SCALINI Piazza Navona 30. ■ 0700-0230 Thu.-Tue. Bus 26,
81. *The best* tartufo *(chocolate ice cream with a hint of truffle) in town.*

NOTA BLU Salita dei Crescenzi 3. ■ 0700-0100 Tue.-Sun. Bus 87,
94. *Home-made ice cream and beautiful view of the Pantheon (see* **A-Z***).*

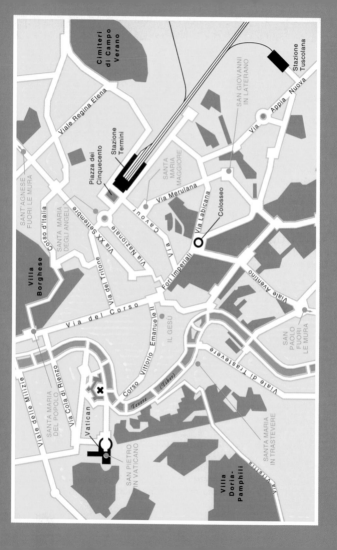

CHURCHES 1

SAN PIETRO IN VATICANO St. Peter's. See VATICAN, **A-Z**.

SAN GIOVANNI IN LATERANO Piazza San Giovanni in Laterano. ■ 0700-1800. Cloister 0900-1300, 1500-1800. M San Giovanni. *The cathedral church of Rome, with a 5thC baptistry and superb 13thC cloister. See* **A-Z**.

SANTA MARIA MAGGIORE Piazza Santa Maria Maggiore. ■ 0700-1900. Loggia 0930-1800. M Termini. ● Church Free, Loggia Inexpensive. *One of Rome's great patriarchal churches, with a stunning 16thC ceiling and, in the loggia, important 13thC mosaics. See* **A-Z**.

SAN PAOLO FUORI LE MURA Via di San Paolo/Via Ostiense 190. ■ 0700-1900. M San Paolo. *Second great basilica after St. Peter's, rebuilt in the 19thC but with earlier remains, including a 13thC cloister.*

IL GESÙ Piazza del Gesù, off Corso Vittorio Emanuele II. ■ 0600-1230, 1600-1915. Bus 56, 60, 62, 64. *Rome's principal Jesuit church. St. Ignatius Loyola is buried here. See* **A-Z**.

SANTA MARIA IN TRASTEVERE Piazza Santa Maria in Trastevere. ■ 0800-1300, 1600-1900. Bus 56, 60, 170. *Originally dating from the 4thC, it has 12th and 13thC mosaics.*

SANTA MARIA DEL POPOLO Piazza del Popolo. ■ 0700-1200, 1600-1900 Mon.-Sat., 0800-1330, 1630-1930 Sun. M Flaminio. *Contains Raphael's Chigi chapel and paintings by Caravaggio. See* **A-Z**.

SANT'AGNESE FUORI LE MURA Via Nomentana 349. ■ 0900-1200, 1600-1800 Mon.-Sat. Bus 36, 60, 63. ● Church Free, Catacombs Moderate. *The burial place of St. Agnes, built over 2nd-3rdC catacombs. Nearby is the 4thC mausoleum of Costanza. See* **A-Z**.

SANTA MARIA DEGLI ANGELI Piazza della Repubblica. ■ 0730-1230, 1600-1830. M Repubblica. *Designed by Michelangelo utilizing some surviving parts of the Terme di Diocleziano. See* **A-Z**.

23

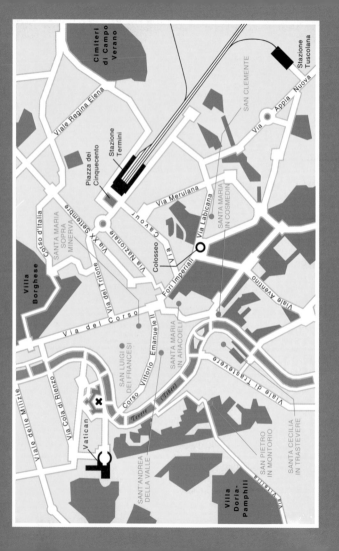

SANTA CECILIA IN TRASTEVERE Piazza di Santa Cecilia.
■ 0700-1200, 1600-1900. Bus 26, 44, 170. ● Church Free, Crypt and earlier remains Inexpensive. *Built over a Roman house and baths, the church has an important fresco of 1293 by Cavallini (see **A-Z**).*

SAN CLEMENTE Piazza San Clemente. ■ 0900-1230, 1530-1800 Mon.-Sat., 1000-1230, 1530-1800 Sun. Ⓜ Colosseo. ● Church Free, Earlier remains Inexpensive. *Beautiful 12thC basilica over a 4thC church and earlier house and temple. See **A-Z**.*

SAN LUIGI DEI FRANCESI Piazza San Luigi dei Francesi.
■ 0730-1230, 1530-1900. Bus 26, 70 to Corso del Rinascimento. *Contains Caravaggio's (see **A-Z**) cycle of paintings of the life of St. Matthew.*

SANTA MARIA IN ARACOELI Piazza d'Aracoeli. ■ 0700-1200, 1600-1730 (summer), 0700-1200, 1530-1730 (winter). Bus 26, 44, 90, 170. *Magnificent frescoes by Pintoricchio (see **A-Z**) and a revered image of the Christ Child. See **A-Z**.*

SANTA MARIA IN COSMEDIN Piazza della Bocca della Verità.
■ 0700-1200, 1600-1900. Bus 28, 29, 90, 92, 94. *The most beautiful medieval church in Rome. See **A-Z**.*

SANTA MARIA SOPRA MINERVA Piazza della Minerva.
■ 0700-1200, 1600-1900. Bus 26, 87, 94. *Rome's only Gothic church.*

SAN PIETRO IN MONTORIO Piazza San Pietro in Montorio, Via Garibaldi. ■ 0700-1200, 1600-1800. Bus 41, 44. *15thC church with frescoes by Sebastiano del Piombo, and Bramante's (see **A-Z**) famous Tempietto in the cloister. See **A-Z**.*

SANT'ANDREA DELLA VALLE Piazza Sant'Andrea della Valle.
■ 0730-1200, 1830-1930 Mon.-Sat., 0730-1245, 1830-1945 Sun. Bus 62, 64, 70. *Splendid Baroque church which is the setting for Act I of Puccini's opera* Tosca.

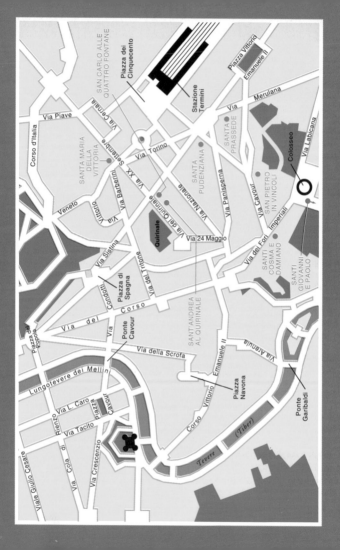

SANT'ANDREA AL QUIRINALE Via del Quirinale 29.
■ 0800-1200, 1600-1900 Wed.-Mon. Ⓜ Barberini. *This oval church of 1671 by Bernini (see A-Z) is a masterpiece of Baroque harmony.*

SAN CARLO ALLE QUATTRO FONTANE Via del Quirinale 23. ■ 0900-1230, 1600-1800 Mon.-Fri., 0900-1230 Sat. Ⓜ Barberini. *Like nearby Sant'Andrea (see above), San Carlo is a tiny Baroque gem, this time by Bernini's great rival Borromini (see A-Z).*

SANTI COSMA E DAMIANO Via dei Fori Imperiali.
■ 0700-1300, 1430-1900. Ⓜ Colosseo.
6thC church with an apse mosaic of outstanding power and vitality.

SANTI GIOVANNI E PAOLO Via San Paolo della Croce, off Via Claudia. ■ 0700-1200, 1600-1800. Ⓜ Colosseo.
Though much altered in the 18thC, this church has fascinating remains of the 5thC basilica built over Roman houses and early Christian tombs.

SANTA MARIA DELLA VITTORIA Via XX Settembre.
■ 0630-1200, 1630-1930. Ⓜ Repubblica.
The Cornaro chapel has Bernini's (see A-Z) sculpture of St. Teresa, the Baroque extravaganza.

SAN PIETRO IN VINCOLI Piazza San Pietro in Vincoli.
■ 0700-1230, 1530-1830. Ⓜ Cavour.
Houses the chains said to have bound St. Peter in Jerusalem and Rome, and Moses by Michelangelo (see A-Z). See A-Z.

SANTA PRASSEDE Via di Santa Prassede 9, off Via Merulana.
■ 0700-1200, 1600-1800. Ⓜ Cavour.
The chapel of St. Zeno has beautiful 9thC Byzantine mosaics.

SANTA PUDENZIANA Via Urbana 161. ■ 0830-1230, 1530-1830 Mon.-Sat., 0900-1230, 1530-1830 Sun. Ⓜ Cavour. *Contains a splendidly lively and delicate 5thC mosaic of Christ and the Apostles with saints Prassede and Pudenziana, two Roman sisters converted by St. Peter.*

Castelli Romani

A one-day excursion to the small towns to the south of Rome which grew up around the defensive castles built by Roman families in the Middle Ages; hence 'Castelli Romani'. Directions are given below for travel by car. However, all the towns can also be reached by bus COTRAL from M Cinecittà and M Anagnina. Trains for Marino, Castel Gandolfo, Albano Laziale, Velletri and Frascati leave from Stazione Termini.

Leave by Porta San Giovanni and take the SS 215 towards Frascati. At the ring road (*raccordo anulare*), turn right on Via Anagnina (SS 511).
27 km – Grottaferrata. Immediately after entering the town, turn right along Corso del Popolo to visit the Abbazia di Nilo (0900-1200, 1630-1800; museum 0900-1230, 1615-1900 Tue.-Sun.), run by Basilian monks who follow the Byzantine rite. Founded in 1004 by St. Nilus, its fortifications were added in the 15thC by Cardinal Guiliano della Rovere, later Pope Julius II. The museum displays illuminated codices, liturgical objects, paintings and enamel-work. The monastery church of Santa Maria has a beautiful 12thC campanile (bell tower) and a Byzantine-style marble portal. The triumphal arch is adorned with 13thC mosaics, and the chapel of St. Nilus contains superb frescoes by Domenichino. From the abbey, turn right and then left through the town onto the SS 216.
31 km – Marino. A beautiful town with splendid views of Lago Albano and Castel Gandolfo. Admire the town hall set in the 16thC Palazzo Colonna, and the 17thC church of San Barnaba. The local white wine is delicious, and there is an annual wine festival (Sagra dell'Uva) on the first Sun. in Oct. Follow the road round Lago Albano.
35 km – Castel Gandolfo. The traditional site of Alba Longa, capital town of the Latin Confederation destroyed by Rome c.600 BC. The small town is famous today as the Pope's summer residence. Continue along the road which is lined with centuries-old oak trees.
39 km – Albano Laziale. This ancient settlement is famous for its white wine and is popular with tourists. Emperor Domitian had a villa here, and Septimus Severus built a fortress and barracks whose *cisternone* (large water tank) is still working. Also of interest are the 12thC church of San Pietro, with a fine campanile, the amphitheatre and the tomb of

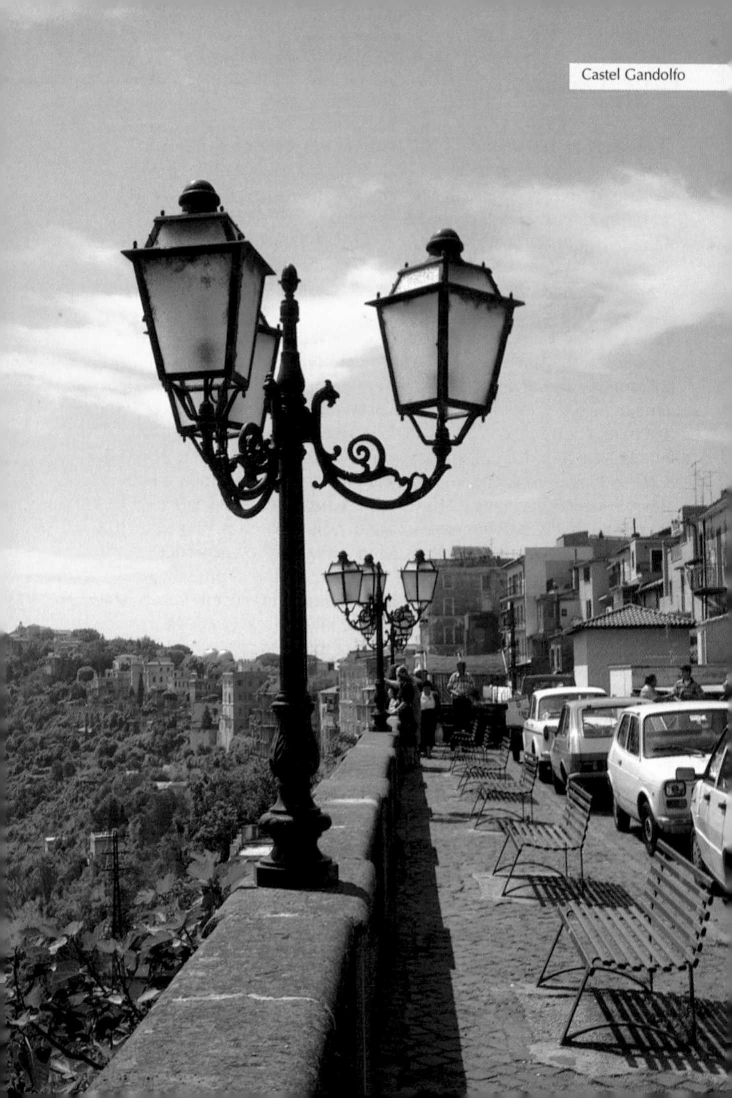
Castel Gandolfo

the Horatii and the Curiatii. Leave the town by Borgo Garibaldi and cross a 300 m-long bridge.

41 km – Ariccia. Visit the lovely Piazza della Repubblica, designed by Bernini (see **A-Z**) in 1665. Continue along the same route.

43 km – Genzano di Roma. On the outer slope of the crater containing Lago di Nemi, this town is famous for the Infiorata, a festival held during Corpus Christi (June), when the main street is carpeted with flowers. Follow Via Appia Nuova (SS 7).

53 km – Velletri. Visit the cathedral of San Clemente (mostly 14th-15thC), and the Palazzo Comunale (16thC), which houses the municipal museum. Return along the road you came in on and turn right, following the signs for Rocca di Papa. Eight kilometres further on, a road to the left leads to Nemi, a picturesque village which is worth a brief detour. Return to the SS 7 and carry on. Turn right onto the SS 218 to Rocca di Papa. About 1 km before the village a small road on the right leads to the top of Monte Cavo (950 m), where a hotel-restaurant sits on the site of the temple to Jupiter Laziale, built by Tarquinius Superbus. From here there are excellent views over the lakes and surrounding countryside.

57 km – Rocca di Papa. A small town situated on the northern slopes of Monte Cavo, and surrounded by beautiful countryside. Head downhill to the SS 216 and turn right, following the signs for Frascati.

63 km – Frascati. Internationally famous for its white wines, Frascati has been popular since Roman times as a holiday resort, and today many rich Roman families keep luxurious villas in the area. Notable sights include: the cathedral of San Pietro with its magnificent Baroque façade by Girolamo Fontana; the Chiesa del Gesù, a 17thC Jesuit church with a façade attributed to Pietro da Cortona and interior frescoes by Andrea Pozzo; and the 17thC Villa Aldobrandini designed by G. della Porta. Return to Rome on Via Tuscolana (SS 215).

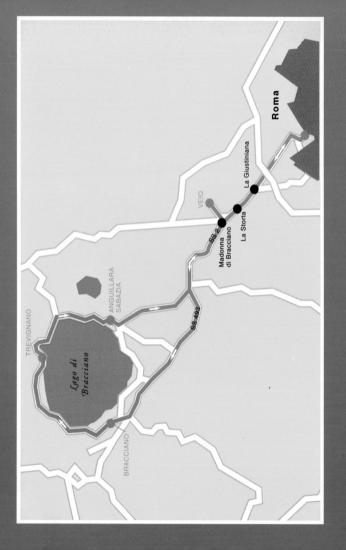

EXCURSION 2

One day. Directions are given below for travel by car. However, all the towns can also be reached by bus COTRAL from Via Lepanto (Ⓜ Lepanto). Trains for Bracciano leave from Stazione Termini.

Leave Rome by Porta del Popolo on Via Flaminia to Piazza Apollodoro. Take Corso di Francia to the right, cross the Tiber and branch left onto Via Cassia Nuova. Follo Via Cassia Nuova through La Giustiniana (14 km) and La Storta (17 km) to Madonna di Bracciano (18 km), and branch left again on Via Claudia to Bracciano.

40 km – Bracciano. The imposing Castello Orsini-Odescalchi (1485) towers above this delightful town, set on the lush hillside above Lago di Bracciano. The castle is a superb example of Renaissance military architecture and has lavishly decorated rooms (guided tours every hour 0900-1230, 1500-1830 Tue.-Sun.). The lake is set in an extinct volcanic crater (as are most of the lakes around Rome). Along the shore are bathing places and restaurants, as well as sailing, motorboat and water-skiing facilities at the various lakeside resorts. From Bracciano follow the lakeside road to Trevignano.

52 km – Trevignano. Visit the fine collegiate church of Santa Maria Assunta with its 16thC frescoes, and take a stroll along the beach. Continue around the lake.

64 km – Anguillara Sabazia. A pleasant medieval town set on a basalt promontory overlooking the lake. See the round tower in the stronghold above the town, the cobbled street leading up to the church of the Assumption, and the monumental town gate with its clock, or just stroll along the tree-lined lakeside promenade where there is a small beach and harbour. Drive south from Anguillara, following the signs for Rome, to rejoin Via Claudia Bracciancese (SS 493). Continue to the junction with Via Cassia and turn left, following signs for Viterbo, then take the first right.

82 km – Veio. The remains of an important Etruscan city, conquered in 396 BC by the Romans after a ten-year siege. See the foundations of the temple of Apollo, where the famous *Apollo of Veio* was found (now in Villa Giulia – see **A-Z**), the frescoes of the Tomba Campana and the remains of the bathing pool. Return to Rome on Via Cassia.

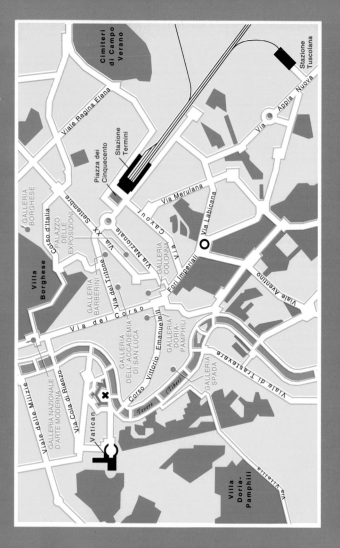

GALLERIA BORGHESE Villa Borghese, Viale dell'Uccelleria.
■ 0900-1900 Tue.-Sat., 0900-1300 Sun. (summer), 0900-1400 Tue.-Sat., 0900-1300 Sun. (winter). M Spagna. ● Inexpensive. *Masterpieces by Bernini (see A-Z), Canova, Raphael (see A-Z), Titian and Caravaggio (see A-Z). See A-Z.*

GALLERIA BARBERINI Palazzo Barberini, Via Quattro Fontane 13. ■ 0900-1400 Tue.-Sat., 0900-1300 Sun. M Barberini. ● Moderate. *The major national collection. Includes Raphael's La Fornarina. See A-Z.*

GALLERIA DORIA-PAMPHILI Piazza Collegio Romano 1a.
■ 1000-1300 Tue. & Fri.-Sun. Bus 60, 62, 87, 88. ● Inexpensive. *The richest private collection in Rome. See A-Z.*

GALLERIA SPADA Palazzo Spada, Piazza Capo di Ferro 3.
■ 0900-1400 Tue.-Sat., 0900-1300 Sun. Bus 26, 44, 60. ● Inexpensive. *Small but interesting collection includes portraits by Titian and Rubens.*

GALLERIA COLONNA Palazzo Colonna, Via della Pilotta 17.
■ 0900-1300 Sat. Closed Aug. Bus 60, 62, 85. ● Inexpensive. *Private collection, including* Portrait of a Nobleman *by Veronese.*

GALLERIA DELL'ACCADEMIA DI SAN LUCA
Piazza dell'Accademia di San Luca 77. ■ 1000-1300 Mon., Wed. & Fri., & last Sun. of month. M Barberini. ● Inexpensive. *Works by Raphael (see A-Z) and Rubens. Spiral staircase by Borromini (see A-Z).*

GALLERIA NAZIONALE D'ARTE MODERNA Villa Borghese, Viale delle Belle Arti 131. ■ 0900-1900 Tue.-Sat., 0900-1300 Sun. M Flaminio. ● Moderate. *Italian and international collection of art from the late 19thC to the present. See A-Z.*

PALAZZO DELLE EXPOSIZIONI Via Nazionale 194.
■ 1000-2100 Mon. & Wed.-Sun. Bus 57, 64, 65. ● Expensive. *Modern art and design exhibitions. The shop sells Italian design items. The building is beautifully lit at night.*

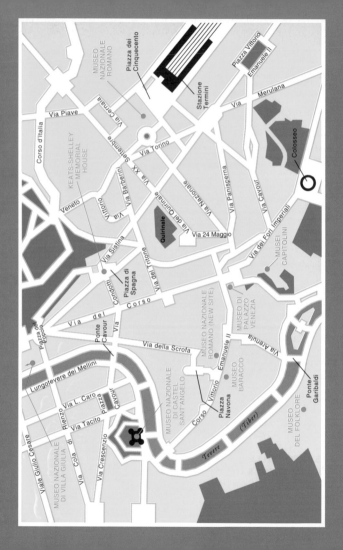

MUSEI CAPITOLINI Piazza del Campidoglio. ■ 0900-1330 Tue.-
Sat. (also 1700-2000 Tue., 2000-2300 Sat., summer, & 1700-2000 Tue.
& Sat., winter), 0900-1300 Sun. Bus 26, 87, 90.● Moderate.
Impressive range of works of art housed in two palazzi. *See* **A-Z**.

MUSEO NAZIONALE ROMANO Viale Enrico de Nicola 79.
■ 0900-1400 Tue.-Sat., 0900-1300 Sun. Ⅿ Repubblica. ● Inexpensive.
*The main archaeological museum, in the process of moving to a new
site at Palazzo Massimo alle Colonne, Corso Vittorio Emanuele II 131
(Bus 46, 62, 64). See* **A-Z**.

MUSEO NAZIONALE DI VILLA GIULIA Piazzale di Villa
Giulia 9. ■ 0900-1400 Tue. & Thu.-Sat., 0900-1930 Wed. Ⅿ Flaminio.
● Moderate. *Great collection of pre-Roman antiquities. See* **Villa Giulia**.

MUSEO NAZIONALE DI CASTEL SANT'ANGELO
Lungotevere Castello. ■ 0900-1300 Tue., Wed., Fri. & Sat., 1400-1800
Mon., 0900-1800 Thu., 0900-1200 Sun. Bus 23. ● Moderate. *Militaria,
paintings, furniture and tapestries. See* **Castel Sant'Angelo**.

MUSEO DI PALAZZO VENEZIA Via del Plebiscito 118. ■ 0900-
1330 Tue.-Sat., 0900-1230 Sun. Bus 44, 46, 60, 70, 81. ● Moderate.
Superb collection of fine and decorative arts, with 13th-15thC tapestries.

MUSEO BARACCO Corso Vittorio Emanuele II 168. ■ 0900-1330
Tue.-Sat. (also 1700-2000 Tue. & Thu.), 0900-1300 Sun. Bus 46, 62,
64. ● Inexpensive. *An important collection of Assyrian, Egyptian, Greek
and Roman sculptures. See* **A-Z**.

KEATS-SHELLEY MEMORIAL HOUSE Piazza di Spagna 26.
■ 0900-1300, 1430-1730 Mon.-Fri. Ⅿ Spagna. ● Moderate. *Keats'
house is now a memorial to these two poets who died in Italy. See* **A-Z**.

MUSEO DEL FOLKLORE Piazza di Sant'Egidio 1b, Trastevere.
■ 0900-1330 Tue.-Sat. (also 1700-1930 Thu.), 0900-1230 Sun. Bus 56,
60. ● Inexpensive. *Dioramas of Roman life in the last two centuries.*

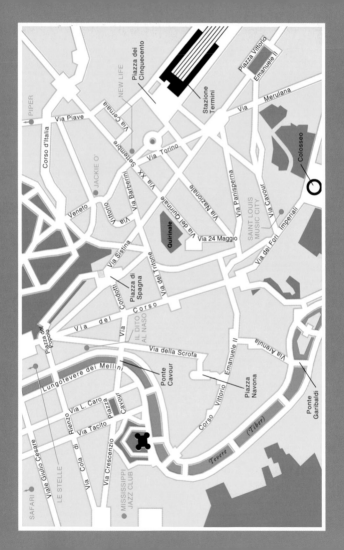

JACKIE O' Via Boncompagni 11.
■ 2200-0300 Thu.-Sat. Bus 58. ● Expensive.
Very elegant but pricey discotheque. Popular with the stars.

MISSISSIPPI JAZZ CLUB Borgo Angelico 16.
■ 1900-0200 Tue.-Sun. M Ottaviano. Bus 98, 808, 881. ● Expensive.
*Rome's lively jazz venue, featuring many of the top names and best
sounds in jazz music.*

IL DITO AL NASO Via del Fiume 4.
■ 2100-0230 Mon.-Sat. Bus 2, 90. ● Expensive.
*This piano bar is a private club but smart dress will guarantee you entry.
Once inside you can enjoy excellent cocktails.*

PIPER Via Tagliamento 9.
■ 2200-0300 Wed.-Sun. (also 1600-1930 Sat. & Sun.). Bus 56.
● Moderate.
*One of Rome's oldest and best-known discos, now popular again with a
youngish set. Live bands and videos.*

SAFARI Via Aurelia 601.
■ 2230-0330 Thu.-Sun. Bus 46. ● Moderate.
Afro and Latin-American discotheque with regular live music.

LE STELLE Via Beccaria 22.
■ 0230-0630 Thu.-Sat. M Flaminio. ● Moderate.
Very late-night disco popular with young people.

NEW LIFE Via XX Settembre 92.
■ 2330-0330 Tue.-Sat. Bus 61, 62, 65. ● Moderate.
Discotheque currently dedicated to house and techno music.

SAINT LOUIS MUSIC CITY Via del Cardello 13a.
■ 2200-0300 Mon.-Wed., Fri. & Sat. M Colosseo. ● Moderate.
*Live music (jazz, blues and R & B) and disco. Frequented by a wide age
range.*

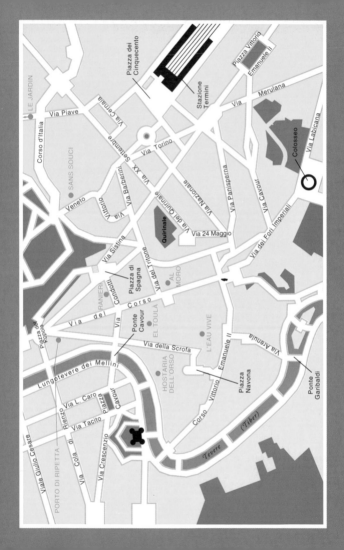

RESTAURANTS 1

SANS SOUCI Via Sicilia 20, tel: 4821814. ■ 2000-0200 Tue.-Sun. Closed Aug. Reservation essential. M Barberini. ● Expensive. *Luxurious, high-class restaurant. Haute cuisine served until late.*

EL TOULÀ Via della Lupa 29b, tel: 6873498/6873750. ■ 1200-1500 Mon.-Fri., 2000-2300 Mon.-Sat. Closed Aug. Reservation essential. Bus 81, 90. ● Expensive. *Considered by many to be the best restaurant in Rome, El Toulà offers delicious Veneto (Venetian) specialities in sumptuous surroundings.*

HOSTARIA DELL'ORSO Via dei Soldati 25, tel: 6864250. ■ 1930-2400 Mon.-Sat. Bus 26, 70, 81, 87, 90. ● Expensive. *Set in a magnificent 13thC palazzo, it is also a piano bar and nightclub.*

RANIERI Via Maria dei Fiori 26, tel: 6791592. ■ 1230-1500 Tue.-Sat., 1930-2300 Mon.-Sat. M Spagna. ● Expensive. *Offers fine traditional Italian cooking in an old-world atmosphere.*

L'EAU VIVE Via Monterone 85, tel: 6541095. ■ 1200-1500, 1900-2300 Mon.-Sat. Closed mid July-late Aug. Reservation essential. Bus 64. ● Expensive. *French restaurant run by nuns in a 16thC palazzo built for Pope Leo X.*

PORTO DI RIPETTA Via di Ripetta 250, tel: 3612376. ■ 1200-1500, 2000-0030 Mon.-Sat. Bus 2, 90. ● Expensive. *Inventive meat and fish dishes for a discerning clientele.*

AL MORO Vicolo delle Bollette 13, tel: 6783495. ■ 1230-1500, 2000-2300 Mon.-Sat. Closed Aug. M Barberini. ● Expensive. *Delicious Roman food in a pleasant and lively setting near the Trevi Fountain. The waiters have a reputation for being the most arrogant in the city.*

LE JARDIN Via G. de Notaris 5, Parioli, tel: 3224541. ■ 1200-1500, 2000-2400 Mon.-Sat. Closed mid Aug. Reservation essential. Bus 56. ● Expensive. *In the five-star Lord Byron Hotel, this is one of the best restaurants in Italy. Refined French and Italian cuisine.*

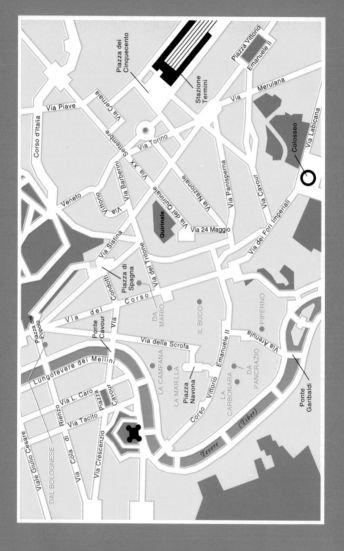

RESTAURANTS 2

DA PANCRAZIO Piazza del Biscione 92, tel: 6861246.
■ 1200-1500, 1900-2400 Thu.-Tue. Reservation essential. Bus 60, 64.
● Expensive. *On the site of the Teatro di Pompeo where Cicero says Julius Caesar (see **A-Z**) was murdered. Excellent Roman cooking.*

LA MAIELLA Piazza Sant'Apollinare 45-46, tel: 6564174/6864174.
■ 1200-1500, 2000-2400 Mon.-Sat. Bus 26, 90, 91. ● Expensive.
An excellent trattoria in a medieval setting, serving specialities from the Abruzzo district.

PIPERNO Via Monte dei Cenci 9, tel: 6542772/6540629. ■ 1200-1500 Tue.-Sun., 2000-2300 Tue.-Sat. Reservation essential. Bus 24, 774. ● Expensive. *Roman-Jewish restaurant, famous for its carciofi alla guidia (artichokes Jewish style).*

LA CAMPANA Vicolo della Campana 18, tel: 6867820/6875273.
■ 1200-1500, 2000-2400 Tue.-Sun. Closed Aug. Bus 81, 90.
● Moderate. *Delicious Roman cooking in this eating house dating back to the 16thC. Try the alicette gratinate (anchovies au gratin).*

LA CARBONARA Piazza Campo dei Fiori 23, tel: 6864783.
■ 1200-1500, 2000-2300 Wed.-Mon. Closed mid Aug. Bus 62, 64.
● Moderate. *Traditional Roman cooking. Superb variety of pasta, fresh fish and desserts.*

DAL BOLOGNESE Piazza del Popolo, tel: 3611426. ■ 1200-1500, 2000-2300 Mon.-Fri. Closed mid Aug. Ⓜ Flaminio. ● Moderate.
Home-made pasta and Bolognese specialities attract fashionable crowd.

IL BUCO Via Sant'Ignazio 8, tel: 6793298. ■ 1200-1500, 2000-2300 Tue.-Sun. Closed mid-late Aug. Bus 64. ● Moderate.
Small, charming restaurant serving traditional Florentine cuisine.

DA MARIO Via della Vite 55, tel: 6783818. ■ 1200-1500, 2000-2300 Mon.-Sat. Closed mid-late Aug. Ⓜ Spagna. ● Moderate. *Tuscan specialities include game (in season) and cannellini (white beans).*

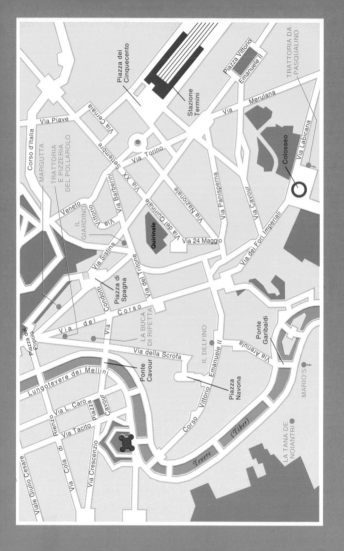

TRATTORIA DA PASQUALINO Via dei Santi Quattro 66, tel: 7004576. ■ 1200-1500, 1930-2300 Tue.-Sun. M Colosseo. ● Inexpensive. *Delicious good-value meals and a friendly atmosphere.*

TRATTORIA E PIZZERIA DEL POLLAROLO Via di Ripetta 4-5, tel: 3610276. ■ 1200-1500, 1900-2300 Mon.-Sat. Pizzeria 1900-2300. M Flaminio. ● Inexpensive. *Good-value pizzas and other main courses.*

MARGUTTA Via Margutta 119, tel: 3235620. ■ 1200-1500, 1800-2300 Tue.-Sun. M Spagna. ● Moderate. *A pleasant vegetarian restaurant set in the fashionable shopping area near to Piazza di Spagna (see* **A-Z***).*

LA BUCA DI RIPETTA Via di Ripetta 36, tel: 3619391. ■ 1200-1500 Tue.-Sun., 2000-2300 Tue.-Sat. Closed Aug. M Spagna. ● Inexpensive. *This friendly trattoria with a lively atmosphere serves typical Roman dishes.*

LA TANA DE NOIANTRI Via della Paglia 1-3, tel: 5806404/ 5896575. ■ 1200-1500, 2000-2300 Wed.-Mon. Bus 44, 56, 60. ● Inexpensive. *Named after the local festival of Noiantri (see* **Events***) held in Trastevere (see* **A-Z***). Traditional Roman cooking, including seafood specialities, in a simple setting.*

IL GIARDINO Via Zucchelli 29, tel: 4885202. ■ 1200-1500, 2000-2400 Tue.-Sun. Closed Aug. M Barberini. ● Moderate. *Simple trattoria serving good-value Roman cooking. Try to get a table in the little garden.*

MARIO'S Via del Moro 53. ■ 1200-1600, 1900-2400 Mon.-Sat. Bus 56, 75, 170. ● Inexpensive. *Delicious food and excellent value in this rather basic-looking restaurant which is always popular with locals.*

IL DELFINO Corso Vittorio Emanuele II 67. ■ 1200-1500, 1900-2300 Tue.-Sun. Closed Aug. Bus 26, 64, 81. ● Inexpensive. *Small restaurant with tavola calda (hot buffet), salad bar and takeaway counter. The roast chicken is recommended.*

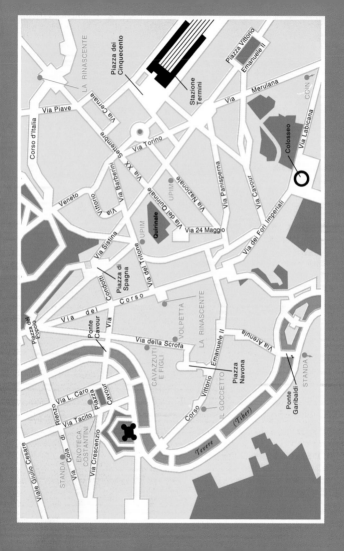

SHOPPING 1

General

COIN Piazzale Appio. ■ 0900-2000 Tue.-Sat., 1600-2000 Mon.
Ⓜ San Giovanni. *Rome's top department store, with five floors of clothes, household goods and electrical appliances. Good value for money.*

LA RINASCENTE Piazza Colonna and Piazza Fiume. ■ 0900-2000 Tue.-Sat., 1600-2000 Mon. Ⓜ Barberini. *Good-quality department stores. The Piazza Colonna branch of this department store sells clothes, perfume, fashion accessories and toys, while the Piazza Fiume branch specializes in household goods.*

STANDA Viale di Trastevere 60 and Via Cola di Rienzo 173.
■ 0900-2000 Tue.-Sat., 1600-2000 Mon. Bus 56, 60, 90, 95.
Department store selling inexpensive household goods. The Via Cola di Rienzo branch has a fine food department.

UPIM Via del Tritone 172 and Via Nazionale 211. ■ 0900-2000 Tue.-Sat., 1600-2000 Mon. Ⓜ Barberini. *This chain store features very cheap clothing and household goods.*

ENOTECA COSTANTINI Piazza Cavour 16b. ■ 0930-1300 Mon.-Sat., 1530-1930 Mon.-Fri. Bus 64, 280. *Worth seeing for the Art Nouveau décor alone. Amazingly well-stocked wine and spirits shop with over 150 types of grappa. It also has a wine bar for tasting.*

VOLPETTA Via della Scrofa 31. ■ 0930-1300 Mon.-Sat., 1530-1930 Mon.-Fri. Bus 87, 94. *Delicatessen with a good selection of Italian cheeses and a bar.*

CAVAZZUTI E FIGLI Via della Scrofa 100. ■ 0930-1300 Mon.-Sat., 1530-1930 Mon.-Fri. Bus 87, 94. *A selection of delicious salamis, truffles and porcini (dried mushrooms).*

IL GOCCETTO Via dei Banchi Vecchi 14. ■ 0930-1300 Mon.-Sat., 1530-1930 Mon.-Fri. Bus 26, 62, 64, 90. *There's a shop with a wide selection of fine wines and oils, and a bar in this attractive old building.*

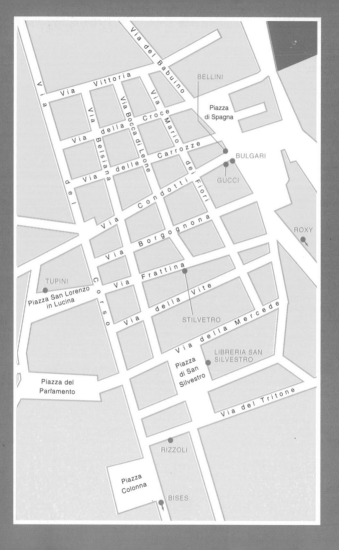

Gifts

RIZZOLI Galleria Colonna at Largo Chigi 15.
■ 1000-1300 Tue.-Sat., 1530-1930 Mon.-Sat. Bus 56, 81, 90.
The largest bookshop in Italy, catering for a wide variety of tastes.

LIBRERIA SAN SILVESTRO Piazza di San Silvestro 27.
■ 1000-1300 Tue.-Sat., 1530-1930 Mon.-Sat. Bus 56, 81, 90.
Bookshop with an excellent arts department, and many bargains.

BULGARI Via Condotti 10.
■ 1000-1300 Tue.-Sat., 1530-1930 Mon.-Sat. M Spagna.
A white marble façade advertises one of the world's greatest jewellers.

GUCCI Via Condotti 8 and 76-77.
■ 1000-1300 Tue.-Sat., 1530-1930 Mon.-Sat. M Spagna.
World-famous range of clothes, luggage, bags, belts and shoes.

BISES Via del Gesù 93.
■ 1000-1300 Tue.-Sat., 1530-1930 Mon.-Sat. Bus 26, 64, 81, 90.
Wonderful collection of luxurious fabrics, set in a 17thC palazzo.

BELLINI Piazza di Spagna 77.
■ 1000-1300 Tue.-Sat., 1530-1930 Mon.-Sat. M Spagna.
Exquisite, expensive, hand-embroidered table linen, sheets, etc.

TUPINI Piazza San Lorenzo in Lucina 8.
■ 1000-1300 Tue.-Sat., 1530-1930 Mon.-Sat. M Spagna.
Specializes in chinaware, but also sells beautiful crystal and silverware.

STILVETRO Via Frattina 56.
■ 1000-1300 Tue.-Sat., 1530-1930 Mon.-Sat. M Spagna.
Good-value Italian tableware and glassware.

ROXY Via XX Settembre 58.
■ 1000-1300 Tue.-Sat., 1530-1930 Mon.-Sat. Bus 36, 60, 62.
There are silk ties galore in this tiny shop. Choose from a wide range of styles, patterns and colours.

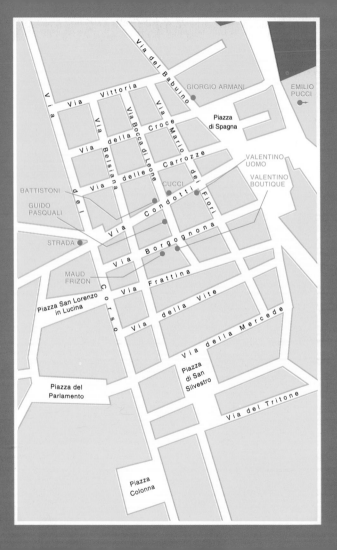

Fashion

CUCCI Via Condotti 67.
■ 1000-1300 Tue.-Sat., 1530-1930 Mon.-Sat. M Spagna.
Expensive, top-quality menswear.

BATTISTONI Via Condotti 57.
■ 1000-1300 Tue.-Sat., 1530-1930 Mon.-Sat. M Spagna.
Classic Italian fashions for men.

VALENTINO UOMO Via Maria dei Fiori 22.
■ 1000-1300 Tue.-Sat., 1530-1930 Mon.-Sat. M Spagna.
Exquisitely tailored suits and shirts for men. Also belts and accessories.

EMILIO PUCCI Via Campania 59.
■ 1000-1300 Tue.-Sat., 1530-1930 Mon.-Sat. Bus 56.
Ready-to-wear clothes from the most famous of Florentine designers.

GIORGIO ARMANI Via del Babuino 102.
■ 1000-1300 Tue.-Sat., 1530-1930 Mon.-Sat. M Spagna.
Inventive fashion from the talented Milanese designer.

STRADA Via del Censo 441-44.
■ 1000-1300 Tue.-Sat., 1530-1930 Mon.-Sat. M Spagna.
Attractive high fashion for men and women at affordable prices.

VALENTINO BOUTIQUE Via Bocca di Leone 15-18.
■ 1000-1300 Tue.-Sat., 1530-1930 Mon.-Sat. M Spagna.
Rome's leading designer provides high fashion for the younger woman.

MAUD FRIZON Via Borgognona 38.
■ 1000-1300 Tue.-Sat., 1530-1930 Mon.-Sat. M Spagna.
The queen of the Paris shoe designers. Very expensive Italian-made footwear.

GUIDO PASQUALI Via Bocca di Leone 5.
■ 1000-1300 Tue.-Sat., 1530-1930 Mon.-Sat. M Spagna.
A shoe designer of great originality, at eminently affordable prices.

San Pietro in Vaticano

SAN PIETRO IN VATICANO St. Peter's, Piazza San Pietro, Città del Vaticano. ■ 0700-1900 (summer), 0700-1800 (winter). Crypt (grottoes) 0700-1800 (summer), 0700-1700 (winter). Treasury 0900-1800 (summer), 0900-1700 (winter). Dome 0800-1800 (summer), 0800-1645 (winter). M Ottaviano. Bus 64. ● Church and Crypt Free, Treasury and Dome Inexpensive. *The seat of Catholicism, built over the tomb of St. Peter and completed in 1626. A place of pilgrimage for Christians and art-lovers. See* **A-Z**.

MUSEI VATICANI Viale Vaticano, Città del Vaticano. ■ 0845-1345 Mon.-Sat. (0900-1600 Easter & July-Sep.). Open last Sun. of month when admission is Free. Closed on religious holidays. M Ottaviano. Bus 64. A special bus runs from Piazza San Pietro through the Vatican gardens to the museums. ● Expensive.
One of the world's greatest art collections, housed largely in the Vatican palace. The collection was started by Pope Julius II in 1503 and contains works acquired or gifted to the papacy down to the present day. Choose itinerary A, B, C or D, depending on how much you want to see (all visit the Sistine Chapel and Raphael's Stanze), and follow the signs. The principal rooms and museums are listed below:
Museo Egizio: *Collection of Egyptian statues, mummies and funerary objects.*
Museo Pio-Clementino: *Priceless classical sculptures, including the* Apollo Belvedere *and the* Laocoön.
Museo Etrusco: *The world's most valuable collection of Etruscan art.*
Stanze di Raffaello (Raphael's Stanze): *Outstanding fresco series by Raphael (see* **A-Z**) *for Pope Julius II. See* **A-Z**.
Appartamento Borgia: *Frescoes by Pintoricchio (see* **A-Z**) *for Pope Alexander VI (1490s).*
Cappella Sistina (Sistine Chapel): *Dominated by Michelangelo's (see* **A-Z**) *masterpieces, the recently cleaned ceiling and the terrifying* Last Judgment. *See* **A-Z**.
Pinacoteca del Vaticano (Art Gallery): *Important paintings by Giotto, Raphael, Leonardo, Bellini, Titian and Caravaggio (see* **A-Z**). *See* **A-Z**.
Biblioteca Vaticana: *Contains over 70,000 codices, manuscripts and early printed books.*

Musei Vaticani

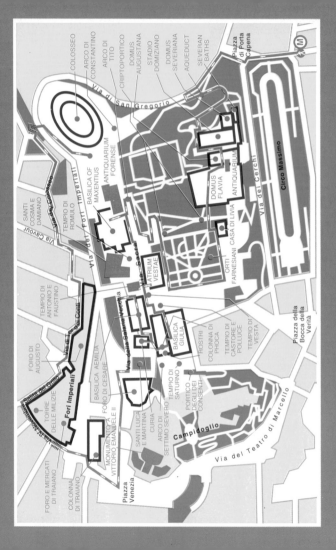

Ancient Rome

Duration: All day; take a picnic lunch. See **ANCIENT ROME 1-3**.

Begin at M Circo Massimo. Turn right out of the Metro and into Piazza di Porta Capena. Ahead on the left is the large area of grassland which was once the site of the biggest racecourse in the ancient world, the Circo Massimo (see **A-Z**). Cross the square and head along Via di San Gregorio towards the Arco di Constantino (see **A-Z**), which is visible in the distance.

About halfway along on the left is the monumental gateway which leads onto the Palatino (see **A-Z**). Take the steps to the left and follow the path which crosses the remains of Nero's aqueduct and climbs past the Domus Severiana and Severan baths to the Stadio Domiziano (96-81 BC). Cross the top of the stadium and continue through the Domus Augustana (the imperial apartments), the Antiquarium, now used to store archaeological finds, and the Domus Flavia, with its courtyard and octagonal fountain, to reach the Casa di Livia, with wonderful wall-paintings. Nearby is the Criptoportico, a semiunderground corridor linking the imperial apartments, supposedly where Caligula was ambushed and assassinated in AD 41.

Walk up to the Orti Farnesiani (Farnese Gardens) and admire the excellent views over the Tiber and the Vatican (see **A-Z**), and down to the Foro Romano (see **A-Z**) and the Colosseo (see **A-Z**). Afterwards, walk down the Clivis Palatinus, past the Arco di Tito, towards the church of Santa Maria Romana. On the right is the Antiquarium Forense, which exhibits archaeological finds from the Forum.

Turn left along Via Sacra. On the right is the basilica of Maxentius or of Constantine, with its three imposing arches, and, just beyond, the 4thC AD Tempio di Romulo, with the church of Santi Cosma e Damiano (see **CHURCHES 3**) behind. Bear left to the circular Tempio di Vesta and the neighbouring Atrium Vestae. The atrium is still visible, with pools surrounded by statues. Continue along Via Sacra past the three Corinthian columns of the Tempio di Castore e Polluce (484 BC) on the left to the Basilica Giulia, built by Julius Caesar (see **A-Z**) in 50 BC. Ahead is the Tempio di Saturno, with eight columns, and up to the left are the twelve columns of the Portico degli Dei Consenti. To the right of the Colonna di Phoca (Column of Phocas) is the Arco di Settimo Severo, erected in AD 203. To the left of it is the Rostri (Imperial Rostra), or the orators'

Foro Romano

Arco di Tito & Colosseo

platform. Ahead is the stern brick façade of the Curia, which once housed the Roman Senate and now displays sculpture reliefs.

From the Curia, turn right past the Basilica Aemilia, then left between this and the Tempio di Antonio e Faustino (AD 141). Exit onto Via della Salara Vecchia. Turn left, passing the 17thC church of Santi Luca e Martina, with each of its storeys dedicated to a different saint, to reach the Foro di Cesare (separated from the other forums by Via dei Fori Imperiali) and on to Piazza Venezia, dominated by the controversial Monumento a Vittorio Emanuele II (see **A-Z**). Turn right around the Colonna di Traiano (see **A-Z**) to reach the steps leading to Via IV Novembre and the Foro di Traiano (see **Fori Imperiali**). Beyond the 13thC Torre delle Milizie, turn right into Salita del Grillo past the Foro di Augusto, and continue down Via di Tor dei Conti, across Via Cavour and along Via del Colosseo to Largo Agnesi and the steps down to the Colosseo.

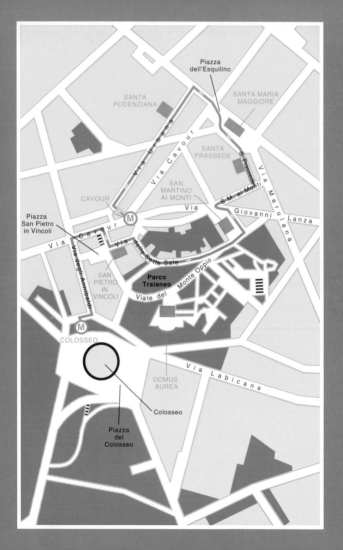

Duration: 2 hr 30 min, excluding visits.

Begin at M Colosseo. From the Metro, climb the flight of steps on the left up to Largo Agnesi. Follow Via degli Annibaldi straight ahead, then turn right under the Palazzo Borgia to Piazza San Pietro in Vincoli with its restored 5thC church (see **A-Z**).

Enter the narrow Via delle Sette Sale on the right on leaving the church and follow it past the Parco Traianeo (with the Domus Aurea visible beyond – see **Nero**) until it merges with Via del Monte Oppio. A little further ahead, on the left, stands the Baroque façade of San Martino di Monti, designed by Gagliardi. The original building dates from c. AD 500 (replacing a 4thC foundation) and was rebuilt in the 9thC.

Turn left out of the church into Via Equizia, cross Via Giovanni Lanza and then turn right into Via di San Martino ai Monti and left down Via di Santa Prassede. Just before the main road is the 7thC church of Santa Prassede (see **CHURCHES 3**), famous for its magnificent 9thC mosaics. Leave the church by the side door and go left to the basilica of Santa Maria Maggiore (see **A-Z**). The interior is breathtaking, and its campanile (75 m) is the highest in Rome.

After visiting the basilica, cross Piazza dell'Esquilino. The obelisk in the centre is one of two which originally stood at the entrance to the Mausoleo di Augusto (see **A-Z**); the other stands in Piazza del Quirinale.

Cross Via Cavour and turn left into Via Urbana. On the right is the 19thC façade of Santa Pudenziana (see **CHURCHES 3**). The original church dates from the 5thC and is one of the oldest in the city. It was built on the site of a house which belonged to a Roman citizen named Pudens, who once gave sanctuary to St. Peter. The church is dedicated to his daughter Pudenziana, and the church of Sant Prassede is dedicated to her sister. The beautifully restored mosaics in the apse depict Christ seated on a golden throne surrounded by his Apostles and the two sisters. Continue along Via Urbana to finish the walk at M Cavour.

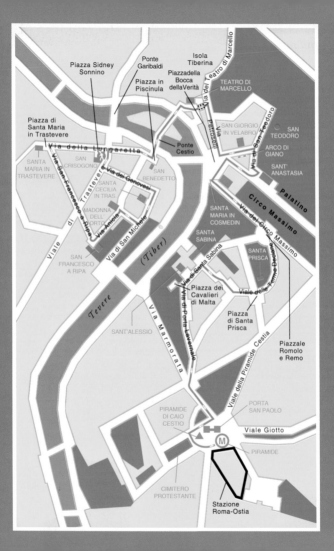

Duration: All day.

Begin in Piazza Sidney Sonnino in Trastevere (see **A-Z**). The church of San Crisogono stands on the piazza, a monumental 12thC building on the remains of a 5thC church. Follow Via della Lungaretta to Piazza di Santa Maria in Trastevere. Its church (see **CHURCHES 1**) was the first to be dedicated to the Virgin Mary (3rdC) and the present building dates from the 12thC.

Go along Via San Francesco a Ripa across busy Viale di Trastevere to the church of San Francesco a Ripa. Inside, in the fourth chapel to the left, is the beautiful statue of the Blessed Louisa Bertoni (1674) by Bernini (see **A-Z**). On the right on leaving the church, Via Anicia leads to the lovely church of Madonna dell'Orto (Our Lady of the Orchard), whose interior is extravagantly decorated on the theme of fruits and flowers.

Go down the street opposite to Via di San Michele, and turn left to reach the imposing tower of Santa Cecilia in Trastevere (see **CHURCHES 2**). Turn left into Via dei Genovesi to Viale di Trastevere, right across Piazza Sidney Sonnino, and right again into Via della Lungaretta, which leads to Piazza in Piscinula and the pretty little church of San Benedetto. Bear left up a small flight of steps towards the Ponte Cestio, which leads across the river to Isola Tiberina (see **A-Z**), with the Roman campanile and Baroque façade of San Bartolomeo. Continue across the Ponte Fabricio on the other side of the island to the Teatro di Marcello (see **A-Z**). Climb down the steps to the right of the theatre, walk across and up to Via del Teatro di Marcello and along Via Petroselli.

Turn left across the street to Piazza della Bocca della Verità. Turn left and pass the ancient Arco di Giano (Arch of Janus). To the left is the simple façade of San Giorgio in Velabro, with a Roman portico and campanile. Unfortunately this church was badly damaged by a recent terrorist bomb.

Turn left into Via di San Teodoro to see the attractively restored 6thC circular church of San Teodoro, and return to the far end of the street where, on the left, is the pleasing façade of Sant'Anastasia, designed by Bernini. Turn right to return to Piazza della Bocca della Verità. On the left is the church of Santa Maria in Cosmedin (see **A-Z**), whose Romanesque campanile overlooks the well-preserved Tempio di Vesta

Santa Maria in Trastevere

(see **ANCIENT ROME 3**) and Tempio della Fortuna Virile (see **ANCIENT ROME 3**) across the way.

Turn left into Via della Greca and Via del Circo Massimo to reach Piazzale Romolo e Remo, which offers broad views over the Circo Massimo (see **A-Z**) and across to the Palatino (see **A-Z**). Cross the square and follow the curving Viale delle Terme Deciane, then turn right into Piazza di Santa Prisca. The church (up the steps to the right) has been restored but it sits on a very ancient site. Cross the square and head towards the summit of the Aventino along Via del Tempio di Diana to the magnificent 5thC church of Santa Sabina. There are excel-lent views over the Tiber from the ter-raced garden beside the church.

Continue along Via di Santa Sabina, past Sant'Alessio (rather poorly renovated during the 18thC) to the lovely Piazza dei Cavalieri di Malta (Square of the Knights of Malta), designed by the 18thC engraver Piranesi. The artist is buried in the small church in the gar-dens of the Priorata

Piazza Santa Maria in Trastevere

di Malta (No. 3), residence of the Grand Master of the Knights of Malta. A unique view of the dome of San Pietro in Vaticano (see **A-Z**) can be gained by peering through the keyhole of the priory gate.

Head downhill on Via di Porta Lavernale and Via Marmorata to the white marble Piramide di Caio Cestio (see **A-Z**) and the Porta San Paolo (see **A-Z**). Behind the pyramid is the Cimitero Protestante (see **A-Z**), a romantic spot worth a visit before finishing the walk at Ⓜ Piramide.

Renaissance Palaces & Churches

Duration: 4-5 hr, excluding visits. Decide in advance which churches and galleries to visit, as most churches close 1200-1530, and most museums and galleries close for the day at 1300 or 1400.

Begin at the Castel Sant'Angelo (see **A-Z**), then cross the Ponte Sant'Angelo (see **A-Z**) and fork left into Via di Panico and left again into Via dei Coronari. This street was laid out in the late 15thC by Pope Sixtus IV to bring light and fresh air into this congested area. Today it is lined with antique dealers and other specialist shops. On the left is San Salvatore in Lauro, which has a lovely Renaissance cloister. Further along (opposite Piazzetta Santa Simeone) turn right into Vicolo di Montevecchio to the piazza and *palazzo* of the same name. Raphael (see **A-Z**) had a studio here.

Head down into Via Arco della Pace and then left, which leads to the church of Santa Maria della Pace, with a façade by Pietro da Cortona. The church contains frescoes by Raphael (*The Sibyls*) and by Baldassare Peruzzi, and to its left is an elegant cloister by Bramante (see **A-Z**). Across and to the left is Vicolo della Pace, which leads to the rear of Santa Maria dell'Anima (German Catholic church), whose campanile is roofed with multicoloured earthenware tiles. Go around the church and across Via dell'Anima into Via dei Lorenesi and on to Piazza Navona (see **A-Z**).

Turn left and left again into Via Agonale, and then right through the archway and down Via di Sant'Agostino to reach the square and church of Sant'Agostino. The church is early Renaissance, but was somewhat insensitively restored in the 18th and 19thC. It contains some masterpieces, notably the *Madonna del Parto* by Sansovino (just inside to the left), *The Prophet Isaiah* by Raphael (second on left), and the *Pilgrim's Madonna* by Caravaggio (see **A-Z**), in the first chapel to the left.

Cross Via della Scrofa, and walk along Via delle Coppelle, then right into Via della Maddalena and Via del Panteone to Piazza della Rotonda, which is overlooked by the impressive façade of the Pantheon (see **A-Z**). Follow, to its left, Via della Minerva to the Gothic church of Santa Maria sopra Minerva (see **CHURCHES 2**). Inside, don't miss the frescoes by Filippino Lippi, and the fine 15thC wooden *Crucifixion* in the innermost right-hand chapel. On the piazza outside stands a small

marble elephant bearing an obelisk by Bernini (see **A-Z**). The obelisk originally belonged to the temple of Isis which stood nearby. Now take Via Piè di Marmo and Piazza Collegio Romano, and turn right into Via del Corso to Piazza Venezia. Next, bear right across the square to visit the church of San Marco, part of the Palazzo Venezia (see **A-Z**). Inside is a Cosmatesque (see **A-Z**) floor, an 11thC mosaic in the apse, and the *San Marco Evangelista* by Melozzo da Forli in the sacristy.

Cross Piazza San Marco and go up Via del Teatro di Marcello beside the imposing Monumento a Vittorio Emanuele II (see **A-Z**), then left up the steps to the unusual brick façade of Santa Maria in Aracoeli (see **A-Z**). Just to its right are steps leading to the majestic Piazza del Campidoglio (see **Campidoglio**). Descend to Via del Teatro di Marcello, turn left down the hill past the remaining three Corinthian columns of the temple of Apollo Sosianus (5thC BC), and turn right down the steps and up into Piazza di Monte Savello in front of the Teatro di Marcello (see **A-Z**).

Enter the former Jewish Ghetto (see **A-Z**) along Via del Portico d'Ottavia past the ruins of the Portico d'Ottavia (see **ANCIENT ROME 2**), which once boasted 300 columns. Continue into Via di Santa Maria del Pianto, cross busy Via Arenula into Piazza Cairoli and then bear right into Via dei Giubbonari, left (opposite Largo dei Librari) into Via dell'Arco del Monte, and right into Via Capo di Ferro. Ahead, in Piazza Capo di Ferro, is the Palazzo Spada (see **A-Z**), built in 1540 and restored by Borromini (see **A-Z**). A little further along Via Capo di Ferro is the Palazzo Farnese (see **A-Z**), now the French embassy.

Cross Piazza Campo dei Fiori and head through Via dei Baullari. On the left, facing Piazza San Pantaleo, is the Piccola Farnesina which houses the Museo Baracco (see **A-Z**). To the left is the Palazzo della Cancelleria, built between 1483 and 1517 by Bramante, and belonging to the Vatican (see **A-Z**). Ahead is the Palazzo Braschi, which houses the Museo di Roma and the Galleria Comunale d'Arte Moderna (see **Museums & Art Galleries**), and further along Corso Vittorio Emanuele II on the left is the Palazzo Massimo alle Colonne, new site of the Museo Nazionale Romano (see **A-Z**). Follow Via della Cuccagna between these last two to end the walk back in the attractive setting of Piazza Navona.

Piramide di Caio Cestio & Foro Romano (inset)

Ara Pacis Augustae: This pagan altar in Via di Ripetta is one of the best-preserved monuments of ancient Rome, consecrated in 13 BC to celebrate peace in the Roman Empire (the Pax Romana), following the victory of Emperor Augustus (see **A-Z**) over Spain and Gaul. The screen surrounding the altar is richly decorated with sculpture reliefs of historical and mythological scenes, and plant and animal motifs. See **ANCIENT ROME 2**.

Arco di Constantino: A triumphal arch dedicated to Emperor Constantine (see **A-Z**) by the Senate and the Roman people in AD 315 after his victory over Maxentius at the Milvian Bridge in the north of the city. Many of its decorative elements, such as the frieze over the central arch, came from earlier monuments. See **ANCIENT ROME 1**, **WALK 1**.

Augustus (63 BC–AD 14): The first Roman emperor. Formerly called Octavian, he was the nephew and heir of Julius Caesar (see **A-Z**). After Caesar's assassination he shared power with Antony and Lepidus, but following the defeat of Antony and Cleopatra at Actium in 31 BC, he established himself as the leading figure in the state and was accepted as such by the Roman Senate, which conferred on him the title of Augustus. He established peace and an effective government, inaugurated an ambitious building programme, including a new forum (see **Fori Imperiali**), and, as patron of such writers as Horace, Virgil and Ovid, encouraged a flowering of literature. See **Ara Pacis Augustae**.

Bernini, Gian Lorenzo (1598-1680): Painter, sculptor, architect, poet – his works epitomize the Baroque style of architecture and sculpture, and were influential throughout Europe. He designed the *baldacchino* (canopy) in San Pietro in Vaticano (see **A-Z**), the famous double colonnade surrounding Piazza San Pietro, and many of the fountains and sculptures that adorn the city. His technical virtuosity and energy, and his ability to convey movement and emotion, make his works among the most admired of his or any age.

Bocca della Verità: Mouth of Truth. This large stone relief of the head of a Roman river-god is in the portico of the church of Santa Maria in Cosmedin (see **A-Z**). In classical times it was probably a cover for a drain or sewer but in medieval times it was moved to its present site for use in trials by ordeal. The suspect (often a woman suspected of infidelity) had to place a hand in the mouth, and it was believed that liars would have their hand bitten off. See **WALK 3**.

Borgo: The medieval district on the right bank of the Tiber whose streets run north and south of Via della Conciliazione. The Borgo (which means 'borough') was originally the site of Nero's (see **A-Z**) circus, where St. Peter suffered martyrdom. The area became popular with pilgrims visiting San Pietro in Vaticano (see **A-Z**), and the district was eventually fortified by the papacy in the 9thC. It was not formally incorporated into the city of Rome until 1586. The area is worth visiting for its ancient streets and houses, two Renaissance *palazzi* – Palazzo Torlonia and Palazzo Penitenzieri – and the church of Santo Spirito in Sassia, founded in AD 726 for Saxon pilgrims.

Borromini, Francesco Castelli (1599-1667): Architect and designer, and the great rival of Bernini (see **A-Z**) in the High Baroque period. The church of Sant'Ivo alla Sapienza (1642-60) is one of his masterpieces and is located inside Palazzo della Sapienza, which now houses Rome's archives, the Archivio di Stato di Roma, at Corso del Rinascimento 40 (0930-1200 Sun., or ask porter for access). Other churches by him include Sant'Agnese in Agone, Piazza Navone and San Carlo alle Quattro Fontane (see **CHURCHES 3**). He also collaborated with Bernini on the Palazzo Barberini, which now houses the Galleria Barberini (see **A-Z**).

Bracciano: See **EXCURSION 2**.

Bramante, Donato (1444-1514): An important Renaissance architect who achieved a beautiful harmony of proportions in his buildings. He is most famous as the architect commissioned in 1505 by Pope Julius II to rebuild San Pietro in Vaticano (see **A-Z**), although his original design was considerably altered by later artists who continued the rebuilding, including Raphael (see **A-Z**), Sangallo and Michelangelo

San Pietro in Vaticano

(see **A-Z**). He also created the Tempietto in the church of San Pietro in Montorio (see **CHURCHES 2**) and the *Cortile del Belvedere* in the Vatican (see **A-Z**).

Caesar, Julius (101-44 BC): Roman statesman and general. At first he was subordinate to Pompey and Crassus, the leading figures in the state, but after a successful military campaign in Gaul (58-51 BC), he led his army to Rome (crossing the Rubicon) and challenged Pompey for supremacy. He pursued Pompey to Egypt, where he installed Cleopatra on the throne and ultimately defeated his rival. After further successful campaigns in Africa and Spain, he returned in triumph to Rome and was appointed Dictator (48 BC). He was responsible for the reconstruction of the forum and the Basilica Giulia (see **Fori Imperiali**). His increasing personal power and ambition caused alarm among Republican opponents in the Senate, and he was assassinated on the ides (15th) of March.

Campidoglio: The Capitol or Capitoline Hill is the most important of the seven hills of Rome and the political and religious centre of the ancient city. Its twin summits were the site of two important temples: Juno Moneta, and Jupiter Optimus Maximus Capitolinus, where newly elected senators were confirmed and victorious generals came to offer thanks to the gods. Today, it is the site of Michelangelo's (see **A-Z**) Piazza del Campidoglio. Steps lead up from Via del Teatro di Marcello past statues of Castor and Pollux, and Emperor Constantine (see **A-Z**) and his son. At the back of the square is the Palazzo dei Senatori (official residence of the Mayor of Rome). On the left is the Palazzo Nuovo, and opposite is the Palazzo dei Conservatori. Together they house the Musei Capitolini (see **A-Z**). In the centre of the square is the bronze equestrian statue of Marcus Aurelius. See **WALK 4**.

Capitol: See **Campidoglio**.

Cappella Sistina: Sistine Chapel. Located in the Musei Vaticani (see **VATICAN**), the chapel was built between 1475 and 1480 by Baccio Pontelli for Pope Sixtus IV. The world-famous ceiling depicts scenes from the Book of Genesis and is one of Michelangelo's (see **A-Z**) masterpieces.

The work was commissioned by Pope Julius II in 1508 and was finished four years later, an achievement of extraordinary artistic vision and physical endurance: Michelangelo painted it lying on his back and largely without the aid of assistants. The main scenes represented are: God separates light and darkness; the creation of the sun, moon and plant life; the Creation of Adam and Eve; the Fall and Expulsion of Adam and Eve from the Garden of Eden; Noah's Sacrifice and the Flood; the drunkenness of Noah. Surrounding the narrative scenes are figures of slaves, and just below the barrel vaulting are the powerful figures of Old Testament prophets and sibyls. The recent cleaning of the ceiling frescoes has understandably caused much controversy. Some scholars argue that while the colours are much brighter, much of the subtlety has been lost and that the backgrounds are now much flatter. In the prophets and sibyls, however, the illusion of three-dimensional figures is much enhanced. Overshadowed by these splendours, but of considerable interest, are the frescoes on the side walls depicting scenes from the lives of Moses (on the right) and Christ (on the left), including Ghirlandaio's *The Calling of Peter and Andrew*, Perugino's *Christ Giving the Keys to St. Peter*, Botticelli's *Moses Killing the Egyptian*, and others by Pintoricchio (see **A-Z**) and Signorelli painted in the 1480s. Above the altar is *The Last Judgment*, with its violent and pessimistic imagery, begun by Michelangelo in 1533, only six years after the disastrous Sack of Rome. Later popes found the nudity shocking and loincloths were painted over the figures. Restoration of *The Last Judgment* is expected to be completed in 1994.

Caravaggio (1571-1610): The greatest Italian painter of the late 16th/early 17thC and a major influence on Baroque painting throughout Europe. His work was often controversial, for example, for the ambivalence and eroticism of some of this earlier works, and in his religious subjects for the stark realism and the use of low-life models to represent biblical characters. Particularly important was his use of light and shadow to dramatic effect. Important examples of his work are in Santa Maria del Popolo (see **A-Z**), San Luigi dei Francesi (see **CHURCHES 2**) and the Pinacoteca del Vaticano (see **A-Z**). He fled Rome in 1606 after killing a man in a brawl, and spent the rest of his life wandering Naples and Sicily.

Cappella Sistina

Castel Gandolfo: See EXCURSION 1.

Castel Sant'Angelo: Begun by Emperor Hadrian (see **A-Z**) towards the end of his reign for use as a family mausoleum, and completed by his successor, Antoninus Pius, in AD 139, one year after Hadrian's death. Because of its strategic position overlooking the Tiber, the mausoleum was used as a fortress from the 3rdC, protecting the northwestern approaches to the city. Its massive, reinforced walls made it a much-appreciated sanctuary for successive popes, and a secret passage (Passetto di Borgo) was built to connect the castle to the Vatican (see **A-Z**). The castle took its name from a chapel dedicated to Sant'Angelo in Nubes, built to commemorate a heavenly vision of the Archangel Michael witnessed by Pope Gregory the Great in AD 590 when leading a procession to San Pietro in Vaticano (see **A-Z**). In 1544 a statue of an angel by Raffaello da Montelupo was placed on the fortress. It was replaced by a bronze angel in 1753, but the marble original can still be seen inside the castle in the Court of the Angel. The mausoleum and fortress were subsequently used as a papal residence (visit the splendid papal chambers), a prison (where the Borgia popes incarcerated their enemies), and a military barracks (during the Napoleonic occupation in the early 19thC). It was restored in the early 20thC and opened to the public as a museum (see **MUSEUMS 2**). Excellent views of the city can be enjoyed from the battlements (the setting for Act III of Puccini's *Tosca*) and the loggias of Julius II and Paul III. See **ANCIENT ROME 1, WALK 4**.

Catacombe di Domitilla: The catacombs were used by pagans and Christians as burial places, and also as secret places of Christian worship. This is probably the largest in Rome, and was established on land originally belonging to Domitilla, a Christian member of the Flavian imperial family. Near the entrance is the great basilica built on the tombs of saints Nereus and Achilleus. From the basilica you enter an ancient plot where members of the imperial family were interred; beyond are over 17 km of passages on four levels, containing many early Christian paintings and inscriptions. See **ANCIENT ROME 3**.

Catacombe di Priscilla: Named after Priscilla, a member of the patrician family gens Acilia and a victim of Diocletian's persecution. The catacombs contain frescoes of biblical scenes and 2ndC representations of the Virgin and Child and the prophet Isaiah, and are some of the oldest such works in existence. See **ANCIENT ROME 3**.

Catacombe di San Calisto: A network of underground passages on four levels, estimated to contain 170,000 graves. Here you will find the famous Cappella dei Papi, where numerous martyred 3rdC popes and bishops are buried. In an adjoining cubicle is the tomb of Santa Cecilia, who also suffered martyrdom in the 3rdC. Her remains are now in the church of Santa Cecilia in Trastevere (see **CHURCHES 2**). There is also an interesting 3rdC passage onto which a number of cubicles open, called the Sacramental Chapels, containing frescoes of Baptism, Confession and the Last Supper. Other notable tombs include those of Pope Eusebius (AD 309-11) and saints Calogeno and Partenio. Via Appia Antica 110. 0830-1200, 1430-1730 Thu.-Tue. Bus 18, 218. Moderate.

Catacombe di San Sebastiano: Visit the 4thC basilica, the Chapel of Symbols containing early Christian inscriptions, and the crypt of St. Sebastian, martyred during Diocletian's persecution. Via Appia Antica 136. 0900-1200, 1430-1700 Fri.-Wed. Bus 118. Moderate.

Catacombe di Sant'Agnese: See Sant'Agnese fuori le Mura.

Cavallini, Pietro (active 1273-1308): Important fresco painter and mosaic artist in Rome. His works are more classical in style than the flatter and more decorative images by contemporaries and as such can be regarded as heralding the Renaissance more than a century later. Major works by him are the mosaics in the apse of the church of Santa Maria in Trastevere (see CHURCHES 1) representing the life of the Virgin and the Madonna and Child, while the church of Santa Cecilia in Trastevere (see CHURCHES 2) has fragments of a fresco of the *Last Judgment* dating from 1293.

Cimitero Protestante: Round the corner from the Piramide di Caio Cestio (see **A-Z**) along Via Caio Cestio is the entrance to the Protestant cemetery. Here many artists and writers are buried, including P.B. Shelley (1792-1822), E. Trelawney (1792-1881), Goethe's son Julius (d.1830), and John Keats (1795-1821), whose tombstone bears the inscription, 'Here lies one whose name was writ in water', added at the request of the poet while on his deathbed. See WALK 3.

Circo Massimo: Circus Maximus. The grand stadium which, together with the Colosseo (see **A-Z**), provided entertainment for the population of ancient Rome. Chariot races and athletics contests held on its 1100 m racetrack drew crowds of up to 200,000 spectators. Today it is a large grassy area amid the traffic. A raised strip marks the top of the *spina*, a wall that once separated the two halves of the racetrack. See ANCIENT ROME 1, WALKS 1 & 3.

Colonna di Marco Aurelio: A marble column 29.6 m high and 3.7 m in diameter which dominates Piazza Colonna. Its shaft is ornamented with a relief rising in a spiral from the base to the enormous Doric capital surmounted by the bronze statue of St. Paul erected in 1589. It was built AD 180-96 to celebrate the victory of Marcus Aurelius over the Macromanni, Samaritans and Quadi. Reliefs in the lower section represent the Germanic War (AD 171-73) and those in the upper the Sarmatic War (AD 174-75); they provide a valuable insight into the

military techniques and life of the period. Inside the column, 190 steps lead to the top. See **ANCIENT ROME 2**.

Colonna di Traiano: Trajan's Column. A marble column standing 38 m high, erected in AD 113 to commemorate Emperor Trajan's wars with the Dacians (AD 101-02, 105-06). The 200 m-long spiral frieze has yielded a great deal of invaluable information about the weapons, uniforms and military tactics of the period. A golden statue of the emperor which once surmounted the column was replaced in the Middle Ages by the figure of St. Peter. See **WALK 1**, **Fori Imperiali**.

Colosseo: Colosseum. This massive but finely-proportioned structure was erected in the time of the Flavian dynasty (AD 69-96, during the reigns of Vespasian, Titus and Domitian), and was originally known as the Amphitheatrum Flavium. It was given its present name after a colossal statue of Nero (see **A-Z**) which stood nearby. It could accommodate 50,000 spectators and was built on the site of a dried-out lake-bed lined with sand and cement to bear the weight. Its inauguration in AD 80 initiated a long history of bloody and brutal animal fights, gladiator contests, athletic games and even mock naval battles, for which the centre of the arena could be flooded. See **ANCIENT ROME 1**, **WALK 1**.

Constantine (c.AD 277-337): Roman emperor, known as
Constantine the Great and as First Christian Emperor. In AD 312 he
defeated his rival Maxentius at the Milvian Bridge in the north of Rome
to become undisputed ruler of the Western Empire, and in subsequent
campaigns defeated other rivals to consolidate his rule. He attributed
his military success to divine intervention and was converted to
Christianity. In AD 313 he issued the Edict of Milan, establishing free-
dom of worship for Christians, which signalled the inevitable demise of
paganism. Several of the early Christian basilicas were begun during his
reign, including the first Basilica di San Lorenzo fuori le Mura, San
Giovanni in Laterano (see **A-Z**) and the first church of St. Peter's on the
Vatican hill. He also completed the secular Basilica of Maxentius in the
forum (see **Foro Romano**), and pieces of his colossal statue can be seen
in the courtyard of the Palazzo dei Conservatori (see **Musei Capitolini**).
For strategic reasons he moved the imperial capital to Constantinople
(Istanbul) in AD 330.

Cosmatesque: Also called Cosmati work. The name given to the
abstract coloured-stone flooring found in many Roman churches. The
mosaic technique uses different types of marble and other stones to
create geometric patterns. As well as being used on floors, it was also
used on tombs, pulpits and other interior areas of churches during the
12th-14thC. The term derives from Cosmate, the name of one of these
mosaic workers. Good examples are at San Clemente (see **A-Z**), Santa
Maria in Cosmedin (see **A-Z**), Santa Maria Maggiore (see **A-Z**) and the
cloisters of Giovanni in Laterano (see **A-Z**).

EUR (Esposizione Universale Romana): This modern suburban
complex 5 km south of the city was begun by Mussolini in 1938 and
was intended as a showpiece of Fascist urban design to be revealed at
Rome's World Fair in 1942. However, World War II intervened and
work did not resume until 1952. The huge Palazzo dello Sport, Via
Cristoforo Colombo, designed by Pier Luigi Nervi for the 1960
Olympics, is perhaps the best example of modern architecture in
Rome. Many of EUR's buildings are now the offices or headquarters of
Italian companies but the area is also a popular residential suburb. The

main attractions are the huge Luna Park amusements (see **Children**), the Museo della Civiltà Romana and Museo Nazionale delle Arte e Tradizioni Popolari (see **Museums & Art Galleries**). M EUR Fermi or EUR Marconi. Bus 93 from Stazione Termini or 97 from Piazza Sidney Sonnino. By car, follow Via Cristoforo Colombo from Porta Ardeatina.

Fontana di Trevi: Trevi Fountain. The largest and most famous fountain in Rome, designed by Nicola Salvi for Pope Clement XII and completed in 1762. Built into the rear of the Palazzo Poli, it is fed by the waters of the Acqua Vergine (built by Agrippa in the 1stC BC), and depicts the figure of Oceanus (Neptune) with sea horses, Tritons and shells. It is traditional for visitors to throw coins into the large basin to ensure their return to the city.

Fontana di Trevi

Fori Imperiali: The Fori Imperiali include the forums of the emperors Julius Caesar (see **A-Z**), where excavations are continuing, and of Augustus (see **A-Z**), Trajan, Nerva and Vespasian. They are situated to the northwest of the earlier Foro Romano (see **A-Z**). Many of the remains are concealed by modern buildings, and by the broad swathe of Mussolini's Via dei Fori Imperiali. Of the Foro di Cesare (54-46 BC), at the foot of the Campidoglio (see **A-Z**), little is visible so far apart from three columns of the temple of Venus Genetrix, which once housed Julius Caesar's collection of sculptures and Greek paintings. All that remains of the Foro di Augusto are three massive Corinthian columns belonging to the temple of Mars Ultor (Mars the Avenger) built in 2 BC. Nearby is the Casa dei Cavalieri di Rodi (House of the Knights of Rhodes), which offers unrivalled views over the five forums. Apart from two Corinthian columns from the temple of Minerva, the Foro di Nerva is almost completely obscured by Via dei Fori Imperiali, as is the Foro di Vespasiano, whose major building was incorporated into the church of Santi Cosma e Damiano (see **CHURCHES 3**). The Foro di Traiano, designed by Apollodorus of Damascus in AD 107 and completed in AD 143, included a triumphal arch, Greek and Latin libraries, the Basilica Ulpia, and a sumptuous temple, although little now remains except the magnificent Colonna di Traiano (see **A-Z**). To the north are the remains of the Mercati Traianei (Trajan's markets), a semicircular, three-tiered complex, once a thriving shopping and commercial centre. See **ANCIENT ROME 2, WALK 1.**

Foro Romano: Roman Forum. Originally a marshy area between the hills of Campidoglio (see **A-Z**) and Palatino (see **A-Z**), the land was drained and gradually developed over a period of 1000 years into the centre of religious, political and commercial life in ancient Rome. From the 8thC the area fell into disuse, the ruined structures were incorporated into

churches and fortresses, or used as quarries, and the area became the
Campo Vaccino, used for cattle pasture, until serious excavations began
in the 18th and 19thC. Today the ruins remain surprisingly evocative of
the power and glory of the ancient city. They include: the Arco di Tito
(Arch of Titus), standing at the eastern end of the site, the oldest surviving
triumphal arch (AD 81), with reliefs depicting Titus' suppression of the
Jewish revolt; the Tempio di Vesta (Temple of Vesta), where the vestal
virgins tended the sacred flame, and the Atrium di Vesta (House of the
Vestals); the Tempio di Antonio e Faustina (Temple of Antoninus Pius and
Faustina), consecrated by the Senate in AD 141; the Tempio di Castore e
Polluce (Temple of Castor and Pollux), first built in 484 BC and restored
by Emperor Tiberius during the 1stC AD; the Tempio di Saturno (Temple
of Saturn), originally dating from c.497 BC, and the one most venerated
by Romans; the Arco di Settimio Severo (Arch of Septimius Severus),
erected in 203 AD in honour of the victories of Septimius Severus and his
sons over the Parthians – this was the prototype for the Arco di
Constantino (see **A-Z**); and the Colonna di Phoca (Column of Phocas), a
14 m-high Corinthian column dedicated to the Byzantine emperor, erected in AD 608, the last monument added. See **ANCIENT ROME 1**, **WALK 1**.

Galleria Barberini: The Galleria Nazionale d'Arte Antica is housed
in the Palazzo Barberini, an imposing Baroque palace by Maderno,
Borromini (see **A-Z**) and Bernini (see **A-Z**), completed in 1633. The main
feature of the *palazzo* is the Salone (Great Hall), with a ceiling fresco by
Pietro da Cortona (*Triumph of Divine Providence*). Among the greatest
treasures of the collection are: *La Fornarina* by Raphael (see **A-Z**), a por-
trait of the artist's mistress (a baker's daughter); a portrait of Henry VIII by
Holbein; a delightful *Madonna* by Filippino Lippi; two magnificent El
Grecos, *The Adoration of the Shepherds* and *Nativity and Baptism of
Christ*; *Venus and Adonis* by Titian; and *Christ and Mary Magdalene* by
Tintoretto. See **MUSEUMS 1**.

Galleria Borghese: The Casino Borghese was completed in 1615 for
Cardinal Scipione Borghese, nephew of Pope Paul V and a great patron
of Bernini (see **A-Z**). It is situated in the eastern part of the Villa Borghese
(see **A-Z**), off Via Pinciana, and contains a priceless art collection. The

ground floor is devoted mainly to sculpture, the first floor to paintings. Among the attractions are: Canova's alluring sculpture of Pauline Borghese, sister of Napoleon, one of his most original works (Room I); Bernini's famous *David*, commissioned by Cardinal Borghese – the features are said to be those of the artist, and legend has it that Borghese himself held the mirror for Bernini while he worked (Room II); in Room III, Bernini's *Apollo and Daphne*, which brilliantly captures Daphne's metamorphosis into a laurel bush while being chased by Apollo; *The Rape of Prosperine*, again by Bernini, in Room IV and *Aeneas, Anchises and Ascanius Fleeing from the Sack of Troy*, in which the sculptor collaborated with his father Pietro, in Room VI. Upstairs, among the many important masterpieces, are: *The Deposition* by Raphael (see **A-Z**) and Pintoricchio's (see **A-Z**) fine *Crucifixion of Saints Jerome and Christopher* in Room IX; a *Madonna with Child* by Andrea del Sarto in Room X; Domenichino's *Sibyl*, also known as *Music*, in Room XII, and his *Diana with her Nymphs* in Room XIV; also in Room XIV, the unforgettable *Boy with a Basket of Fruit* and *David and Goliath* by Caravaggio (see **A-Z**); and Titian's masterpiece, *Sacred and Profane Love*, in Room XX. See **MUSEUMS 1**.

Galleria Doria-Pamphili: The Pamphili and Doria families' art collection is exhibited in the Palazzo Doria where they still live. Among the art treasures are: Titian's *Spain Succouring Religion* and *Salome*; three outstanding paintings by Caravaggio (see **A-Z**) – *St. Mary Magdalen*, *St. John the Baptist* and *The Rest on the Flight into Egypt*; Alessandro Algardi's bust of Olimpia Maidalchini, sister-in-law of Pope Innocent X, whose own portrait by Velázquez can be seen further along the hall; several exquisite 17thC landscapes by Claude Lorraine; and *The Flight into Egypt* by Annibale Carracci (c.1604). See **MUSEUMS 1**.

Galleria Nazionale d'Arte Antica: See **Galleria Barberini**.

Galleria Nazionale d'Arte Moderna: An important collection of 19th and 20thC Italian sculpture and painting, including works by the Italian Impressionists (Macchiaioli), Futurists such as Umberto Boccioni, and Metaphysical artists like Giorgio de Chirico. See **MUSEUMS 1**.

Hadrian (AD 76-138): Emperor (117-38) notable as a great builder, traveller and lover of art and philosophy. In Rome he was responsible for the Castel Sant'Angelo (see **A-Z**) and the Pantheon (see **A-Z**). He also built great frontier fortifications, including the famous wall in Britain and the Limes in Germany. During his travels he visited practically every province of the empire, and was especially fond of Athens and the culture of Classical Greece, as is evident in his final great project, the magnificent Villa Adriana (see **A-Z**) near Tivoli.

Il Gesù: Built 1568-84 as the flagship of the Counter-Reformation, this church became a model for Jesuit churches all over Europe. The façade was designed by Giacomo della Porta, and the incredibly rich interior decoration is by Vignola. See the magnificent fresco of *The Triumph of the Name of Jesus* by Giovanni Battista Gaulli on the ceiling of the nave, and the opulent tomb of St. Ignatius Loyola by Andrea Pozzo, which is topped by the largest known piece of lapis lazuli. Gilded sculptures, coloured marble and skilful trompe l'oeil paintings make Il Gesù the prototype of the early Baroque style. See **CHURCHES 1**.

Isola Tiberina: The island is linked to Trastevere (see **A-Z**) on the right bank by the Ponte Cestio, and to the Cenci district on the left bank by the ancient Ponte Fabricio (built in 62 BC). It was the site of the temple of Aesculapius (the god of medicine), after a serpent, which had been brought to Rome from Epidaurus in Greece, supposedly cured the great plague of 291 BC, and subsequently chose the island as its home. Among the notable sights here are the medieval Torre dei Caetani, and the beautiful church of San Bartolomeo and its peaceful piazza. See **ANCIENT ROME 3, WALK 3**.

Jewish Ghetto: The Jewish community in Rome was established at least a century and a half before the birth of Christ. Early on Jews settled on Isola Tiberina (see **A-Z**) and in the Trastevere (see **A-Z**) district, but by medieval times many of them had moved across the river. In 1555 Pope Paul IV created the Jewish Ghetto in the small area on the right bank of the Tiber opposite Isola Tiberina and forced all Jews to live there. The area extended from the Teatro di Marcello (see **A-Z**) along Via del Portico d'Ottavia and Via Reginella, and across Via Arenula towards Via Capo di Ferro. The walls of the Ghetto were finally torn down during the Liberation of Rome in 1870, when Jews were given the same rights as other citizens. A large new synagogue was built in 1904 on Lungotevere Cenci, which also houses a Jewish museum, Museo di Arte Ebraica (see **Museums & Art Galleries**). The narrow streets of the ghetto are still evocative and there are a number of Roman Jewish restaurants in the area (see **RESTAURANTS 2**). See **WALK 4**.

Keats-Shelley Memorial House: The house where the English poet John Keats (1795-1821) resided for a time in the early 19thC with his companion Joseph Severn is now a library and museum containing memorabilia of Keats and his fellow poet Percy Bysshe Shelley (1792-1822), who both died in Italy and are buried in the Cimitero Protestante (see **A-Z**). You can visit Keats' bedroom and see his death mask. See **MUSEUMS 2**.

Largo di Torre Argentina: Until the 1920s this square was a maze of narrow streets and old buildings which were cleared for the excavation of the remains of a group of Roman temples, at least one of which dates back to the 3rd or 4thC BC. They are, therefore, among the earliest buildings so far excavated in Rome. The Teatro Argentina on the west side of the square was the venue for the first performance of Rossini's *Barber of Seville* (1816), which was booed by the audience.

Mausoleo di Augusto: This large cylindrical marble tomb with a conical earthen mound on top reaches a height of 44 m and is surrounded by cypress trees. It was built by Emperor Augustus (see **A-Z**) for himself and members of the Julio-Claudian family. However, it fell into disrepair and was used in the 12thC as a fortress by the Colonna family, as a quarry for its travertine stone, and in the later 19thC as a concert hall and circus. Piazza Augusto Imperatore. Bus 90, 95. See **WALK 2**.

Michelangelo (1474-1564): Most famous as the painter of the Cappella Sistina (see **A-Z**), although he began his artistic career as a

sculptor. He was also an architect,
draughtsman and poet. He spent his life
in Florence and Rome working alternate-
ly under the patronage of the Medicis
and Pope Julius II. In Rome he created
the famous *Pietà* in San Pietro di
Vaticano (see **A-Z**) in 1499, and then
embarked on two massive projects for
Pope Julius II – the Sistine ceiling (1508-
12) and the tomb of Pope Julius, though
only the figure of Moses (1513-16) is by
the master himself. It is now in San Pietro

Pietà

in Vincoli (see **A-Z**). He worked in Florence 1516-34, then returned to
Rome to work on *The Last Judgment* in the Sistine (1536-41). There is a
marked difference in the style between Michelangelo's early works and
The Last Judgment. Its darker tonality and crowded composition have
been interpreted as a reflection of the artist's personal pessimism, and
indeed the flayed skin on the face of St. Bartholomew (to the right of
Christ) is said to be a self-portrait. His architectural achievements
include Piazza degli Campidoglio (see **Campidoglio**), the dome of St.
Peter's and the Basilica Santa Maria degli Angeli (see **A-Z**).

Monumento a Vittorio Emanuele II: Built between 1885 and
1911, this conspicuous marble monument (135 m long and 70 m high),
known locally as 'the wedding cake', overlooks Piazza Venezia and
commemorates the first king of a united Italy (d.1878). On the lower
terrace are the Tomb of the Unknown Soldier and Altare della Patria
(Altar of the Fatherland). The upper terrace commands superb views
over the city. See **WALKS 1 & 4**.

Mura Aureliane: A wall measuring 19 km in circumference which
surrounds the ancient city. It was built AD 272-79 by Emperor Aurelian
to protect Rome from the Alemanni, whom he had defeated a few years
previously. Today the wall encloses one tenth of the population of the
city. It is best seen between Porta San Paolo (see **A-Z**) and Porta Latina
in the south, and Porta Pinciana to the northwest. See **ANCIENT ROME 3**.

Musei Capitolini: An important collection of sculpture and painting housed in two *palazzi* on either side of Michelangelo's (see **A-Z**) Piazza del Campidoglio. The Palazzo Nuovo, on the left, has mostly classical statuary, notably the *Capitoline Venus*, a Roman copy of a beautiful Greek original, the poignant *Dying Gaul*, and the *Marble Faun*. There is also the Room of the Emperors, featuring 65 busts of Roman emperors, politicians and philosophers. In the courtyard fountain is the statue of Marforio, a river-god. Across the square, in the Palazzo dei Conservatori, you can find the symbol of Rome, the *Capitoline She-Wolf*, in the Sala della Lupa. The wolf is a 6thC BC Etruscan bronze; Romulus and Remus are 15thC additions. See too the *Spinario*, the boy plucking a thorn from his foot. The Pinacoteca Capitolina (in the same building) houses a number of masterpieces by Titian, Caravaggio (see **A-Z**), including the superb *St. John the Baptist*, Guercino (*Burial and Reception into Heaven of St. Petronilla*), Rubens and Van Dyck. The stone head, hand and foot lying in the courtyard are all that is left of a colossal statue of Emperor Constantine (see **A-Z**). The museums are spectacularly floodlit 2030-2300 Sat. See **MUSEUMS 2**.

Musei Vaticani: Vatican Museums. See **VATICAN**.

Museo Baracco: A small collection of Roman, Greek, Assyrian, Egyptian and Etruscan sculpture presented to the city by Baron Giovanni Baracco in 1902. The collection is housed in the Palazzo Piccola Farnesina, designed by Antonio da Sangallo the Younger in 1523 for the French Cardinal Thomas Le Roy. See **MUSEUMS 2**, **WALK 4**.

Museo Nazionale Romano: A large and important collection of Roman antiquities currently housed in part of the Terme di Diocleziano (see **A-Z**), adjacent to the church of Santa Maria degli Angeli (see **A-Z**). Among the sculptural treasures are the magnificent *Ludovisi Throne* (5thC BC), decorated with a relief depicting the birth of Aphrodite; the *Daughter of Niobe* (Greek 5thC BC); *The Discus Thrower*, a copy of the famous Greek statue by Myron; and the *Girl of Anzio* (Greek 4thC BC), unearthed at Anzio in 1878. There is also an important collection of frescoes and mosaics recovered from the Palatino (see **A-Z**). See **MUSEUMS 2**.

Nero (AD 37-68): Convinced of his artistic genius and preoccupied with composing music and poetry rather than governing, his rule (58-68) degenerated into a reign of terror and debauchery – he murdered both his wife and mother. He is thought to have been responsible for the great fire of AD 64, for which he blamed the Christians and made them suffer cruelly. Outlawed by the Senate for political failures, he committed suicide. His Domus Aurea (see **WALK 2**) was one of the most sumptuous of imperial residences, and the Colosseo (see **A-Z**) was named after the colossal statue of him which once stood near the site of the Circo Massimo (see **A-Z**).

Ostia Antica: 25 km southwest of Rome are the remains of this ancient port, a 'must' for anyone with an interest in ancient history and archaeology. Founded c.300 BC, it soon became a prosperous trading centre supplying the capital with foodstuffs, and main base of the Roman fleets that helped to conquer the Mediterranean world. Ostia fell into decline in the 4thC and, after a great flood in 1575, when the Tiber changed its course, the remains of the city were buried in sand. Excavations during the 19th and 20thC have revealed invaluable evidence of day-to-day life in ancient Rome. Works of art recovered from the site are on display in the Museo di Ostia near the Casa dei Dipinti (House of the Painters). Also on the site are the Terme di Nettuno with floor mosaics; Piazzale delle Corporazioni, where the merchants' offices were located; a theatre, where performances are held in summer; the Casa di Diana, a surprisingly modern-looking apartment block; and the forum. Further west are the Domus di Amore e Psiche (House of Cupid and Psyche) and the baths of the Seven Sages (with lavish mosaics). South of the forum is the Domus dei Pesci (a Christian house) and the Capoune del Pavone (Peacock Inn), an ancient wine shop. Trains leave for Ostia Antica from Stazione Ostiense.

Palatino: According to legend, it was on this hill that Romulus first marked out the limits of the city with his plough in 753 BC. It was chosen by the subsequent rulers of the Republic and empire as the site of their sumptuous palaces, lavishly decorated with frescoes and marble sculptures. See **ANCIENT ROME 1**, **WALKS 1 & 3**.

Palazzo Barberini: See Galleria Barberini.

Palazzo Borghese: This palace was designed by Vignola in 1560 and completed by Ponzio in 1614 as the summer residence of Cardinal Camillo Borghese, who later became Pope Paul V (1605-21). Known as 'Il Cembalo' (The harpsichord) because of its unusual shape, it housed the family's magnificent art collection until it was moved to the Casino Borghese in 1891 (see **Galleria Borghese**). Piazza Borghese. Spagna.

Palazzo Doria: See Galleria Doria-Pamphili.

Palazzo Farnese: The most impressive Renaissance palace in the city. It was begun by Antonio da Sangallo the Younger in 1514 and taken over by Michelangelo (see **A-Z**) in 1546. The first floor is decorated with superb frescoes by Annibale Caracci. It has been the home of the French embassy since 1871 and is not open to the public. Piazza Farnese. See **WALK 4**.

Palazzo Piccola Farnesina: See Museo Baracco.

Palazzo del Quirinale: This palace was begun in 1574 by Flaminio Ponzio and extended in stages by Fontana, Maderno, Bernini (see **A-Z**) and Fuga. In 1592, when Clement VIII moved here from the Vatican (see **A-Z**), the Quirinale became the favourite summer residence of the popes. Since 1947 it has been the official residence of the Italian president. For permission to visit, apply to the Ufficio Intendenza, Palazzo Quirinale, Roma 00137. Piazza del Quirinale. M Barberini.

Palazzo Spada: Originally dating from 1540, this palace was restored by Borromini (see **A-Z**) in 1632 – his trompe l'oeil colonnade which links the two interior courtyards is its most interesting feature. It has been the seat of the Italian Council of State since 1889 and also houses the Galleria Spada (see **MUSEUMS 1**), a small collection of 17th and 18thC paintings assembled by Cardinal Bernardino Spada (1594-1661) and his family. See **WALK 4**.

Palazzo Venezia: One of the earliest palaces to be built in Rome, it was begun c.1455 for Cardinal Pietro Barbo, afterwards Pope Paul II (1464-71). From 1564 to 1797 it was the property of the Republic of Venice, while Mussolini later used it as his official residence, and delivered speeches from the balcony overlooking the piazza. The Museo di Palazzo Venezia (see MUSEUMS 2) contains medieval and Renaissance paintings, sculptures, tapestries, ceramics and silver. See WALK 4.

Pantheon: One of the best preserved and most impressive examples of ancient Roman architecture. It was built by Emperor Hadrian (see A-Z) in AD 120-25 on the site of an earlier monument erected in 27 BC by Consul Marcus Agrippa. The emperor was modest enough to retain the original inscription, 'M. AGRIPPA L. F. COS TERTIUM FECIT' (Marcus Agrippa, son of Lucius, Consul for the third time, built this). At the entrance is an impressive portico with 16 granite columns and huge bronze doors. Its many treasures, mainly bronze and marble sculptures, have been plundered long since, but the building itself, and the amazing dome, remain much as they were nearly 2000 years ago. The dome, 43 m across, is larger than that of San Pietro in Vaticano (see A-Z), and the sunlight streaming through the oculus at the dome's apex lends a unique atmosphere to the interior. The monument was Christianized by Pope Boniface IV in AD 608, and dedicated to the martyrs whose bones were brought from the catacombs and reburied here. The Italian kings Vittorio Emanuele II and Umberto I, and the artist Raphael (see A-Z), are also interred here. See ANCIENT ROME 1, WALK 4.

Piazza Navona: One of the most popular squares in Rome, sited on the ancient Circus Agonalis (Domitian's athletics stadium). It is notable for the Fontana dei Quattro Fiumi (Fountain of the Four Rivers) by Bernini (see A-Z) and the church of Sant'Agnese in Agone by Borromini (see A-Z). In the Middle Ages it was popular for jousting, water pageants and horse races, and the carnival atmosphere persists as large crowds gather among the fountains to watch the various street artists and traders, or sit and chat in the cafés lining the square. See WALK 4.

Pantheon

Piazza di Spagna: The square takes its name from the Palazzo di Spagna, built in the 17thC to house the Spanish ambassador to the Vatican (see **A-Z**). Today it is a popular meeting point for visitors (and for crowds of young Romans too). It is best admired from Via Condotti, or from the top of the Scalinata della Trinità dei Monti (Spanish Steps) in front of the church of Trinità dei Monti (see **A-Z**). The steps were built by Francesco de Santis between 1723 and 1726, and are usually crowded with tourists. The boat-shaped fountain was the work of Bernini's father, who supposedly conceived the idea when a boat was stranded here after the Tiber flooded.

Pinacoteca del Vaticano: The art gallery of the Vatican (see **A-Z**) was created by Pope Pius at the end of the 18thC and contains an important collection displayed in chronological order from the 11thC to the 19thC. Outstanding works include the *Stefaneschi Altarpiece*, painted for the earlier church of St. Peter's and attributed to Giotto (1266/67-1337), the most important precursor of the Italian Renaissance; the *Transfiguration of Christ*, Raphael's (see **A-Z**) last major work (1517-20), finished by his pupil Giulio Romano, as well as two earlier Raphael paintings, the *Coronation of the Virgin* and the *Madonna di Foligno*; a series of beautiful 16thC Brussels tapestries originally for the Cappella Sistina (see **A-Z**) from designs by Raphael; a fascinating late work, *St. Jerome*, by Leonardo; and Caravaggio's (see **A-Z**) *Deposition of Christ*, a powerful composition of 1600-04. See **VATICAN**.

Pincio: Public gardens laid out by Giuseppe Valadier in 1809-14 above the Piazza del Popolo (see **A-Z**) on land owned by the Pinci family (4thC). The view from the gardens over the piazza and the centre of the city is superb.

Pintoricchio, Bernardino (c.1454-1513): Also spelt Pinturicchio. Born in Perugia, Pintoricchio came to Rome in the 1480s to assist Perugino, Raphael's (see **A-Z**) master, on the wall frescoes for the Cappella Sistina (see **A-Z**). In the 1490s he carried out the fresco decoration of the Appartamenti Borgia at the Vatican (see **VATICAN**). Other important fresco series are in Santa Maria del Popolo (see **A-Z**) and Santa Maria in Aracoeli (see **A-Z**). His works are characterized by rich colouring and a strong decorative element.

Piramide di Caio Cestio: The marble tomb of Tribune Caius Cestius, built in 12-11 BC, and later incorporated with the Porta San Paolo (see **A-Z**) into the Mura Aureliane (see **A-Z**). The pyramid is 22 m square and 27 m high, and was (according to the inscription) erected in 330 days. See ANCIENT ROME 3, WALK 3.

Ponte Sant'Angelo: The most attractive of Rome's ancient bridges, built by Hadrian (see **A-Z**) in AD 134 (the three central arches survive from this period) to connect the Mausoleo di Adriano (see **Castel Sant'Angelo**) to the old city. The ten statues of angels were added by Bernini (see **A-Z**) and his school in 1669-71. The bridge is a favourite spot with street traders. See WALK 4.

Porta Maggiore: A city gate built in AD 52 by Emperor Claudius at the point where Via Prenestina and Via Labicana passed under two aqueducts, the Acqua Claudia and the Anio Novus. It was later incorporated into the Mura Aureliane (see **A-Z**). Via Prenestina and Via Casilina.

Porta Pia: Built 1561-65, this is one of the last masterpieces by Michelangelo (see **A-Z**). The exterior was restored in the 19thC. There is a military museum (Museo Storico dei Bersaglieri) housed in the outer sections. Via XX Settembre and Via Nomentana.

Porta San Pancrazio: Once the starting point for Via Aurelia, it was erected in the 17thC by Pope Urban VIII and rebuilt in 1854 by Pius IX after it was badly damaged by fighting between Garibaldi and the French. Via Aurelia.

Porta San Paolo: Originally called the Porta Ostiense (3rdC AD), the gate is flanked by defensive towers built in the 6thC. Inside, the Museo della Via Ostiense illustrates the history of this important Roman thoroughfare. See WALK 3.

Porta San Sebastiano: Undoubtedly the best-preserved of the city gates (5thC AD). Flanked by its two imposing towers, it leads to Via Appia Antica (see **A-Z**).

Raphael (1483-1520): Born in Urbino, Raffaello Sanzio became, during the first two decades of the 16thC, one of the three major artists of the Italian High Renaissance. The other two were Leonardo da Vinci and Michelangelo (see **A-Z**), and of the three, Raphael is probably the most easily appreciated for the sheer beauty of his works. In 1508 Pope Julius II called him to Rome (where he remained for the rest of his short life) to decorate the private papal apartments, the Vatican *Stanze* (see **A-Z**), generally considered his most important works. These and other major paintings, such as the *Galatea* in the Villa Farnesina (see **A-Z**), epitomize Renaissance ideas of harmony and ideal beauty. In 1514 Raphael succeeded Bramante (see **A-Z**) as architect of St. Peter's and in 1516 designed the Chigi burial chapel at Santa Maria del Popolo (see **A-Z**).

San Clemente: Originally built over a 3rdC shrine of Mithras (itself housed in a 1stC domus) in the 4thC, it was later destroyed and a new basilica erected by Pope Pascal II (1099-1118). The triumphal arch and apse of the upper church are richly decorated with mosaics of biblical scenes. There is also a beautiful Cosmatesque (see **A-Z**) floor and enclosed choir, while the chapel of St. Catherine (on the left) contains frescoes by Masolino (1425). The lower church (4thC) contains a series of Romanesque (8th-12thC) wall-paintings. On the lowest level are the partial excavations of the 1stC domus and Mithraic temple. See CHURCHES 2.

San Giovanni in Laterano: This basilica is the cathedral church of Rome, and the seat of the Pope in his role as the Bishop of Rome. Very little remains of the original 4thC basilica, as this church has suffered more than any other in the city from the ravages of fires, sackings and earthquakes, as well as a recent bomb attack by terrorists. Its present appearance dates from the 17th and 18thC. The Baroque façade was designed by Alessandro Galilei (c.1735), and the interior by Borromini (see **A-Z**) in 1650. Its notable features include: the bronze doors, taken from the Curia in the Foro Romano (see **A-Z**); the superb timber ceiling; the 13thC mosaics in the apse by Jacopo Torriti; the bronze tomb of Martin V; and the magnificent Cosmatesque (see **A-Z**) work in the cloisters. See **CHURCHES 1**.

San Pietro in Montorio: Founded before the 9thC on the supposed site of St. Peter's crucifixion (wrongly sited on the Gianicolo according to medieval legend), it was rebuilt after 1481 for King Ferdinand IV of Spain by Baccio Pontelli. The church is chiefly notable for the Tempietto (a circular, columned building) added by Bramante (see **A-Z**) in 1502 in the small courtyard to the right of the church, a masterpiece of High Renaissance architecture. See **CHURCHES 2**.

San Pietro in Vaticano: St. Peter's. The seat of Roman Catholicism visited by pilgrims and art-lovers from all over the world. In 1505 Pope Julius II appointed Bramante (see **A-Z**) as architect of the new St. Peter's to replace the original 4thC basilica erected by Constantine (see **A-Z**) near the site of the Apostle's martyrdom (c.AD 64). Bramante's Greek cross design remained incomplete at his death in 1516, and the work was taken over by Raphael (see **A-Z**), Peruzzi and Antonio da Sangallo the Younger until the intervention of Michelangelo (see **A-Z**), whose simple design of a square cross with dome superseded competing plans. Only the drum of the dome was completed before he died, and the finished design owes much to Giacomo della Porta. In 1605 Paul V commissioned Carlo Maderno to add a nave and façade, and the church was finally completed in 1626 and consecrated by Urban VIII. From the central balcony on the façade the Pope delivers his *urbi et orbi* blessing (see **Events**). The portico contains five entrances to the church, the Porta Santa being opened only in a Holy Year. The approach to St. Peter's is made all the more dramatic by the inspired design of the Piazza San Pietro, enclosed by Bernini's (see **A-Z**) masterpiece, an oval colonnade four columns deep, surmounted by 140 statues of saints. In the centre is an obelisk erected by Domenico Fontana (1586), flanked by two fountains by Maderno (1614) and Bernini (1677). Inside, the first chapel to the right contains Michelangelo's famous *Pietà* (1499), protected by special glass since being attacked by an assailant with a hammer in 1972. The Baroque interior is largely the work of Bernini, whose magnificent bronze *baldacchino* (canopy) towers above the high altar. In the apse is Bernini's bronze Throne of St. Peter flanked by patristic figures, and below are the tombs of Paul III to the left (G. della Porta, 1551-75), and of Urban VIII to the right (Bernini, 1642-47). Notable sculptures in the left aisle include: the tomb of Alexander VII (Bernini, 1672-78); the Cappella della Colonna (1646-50); the tomb of Leo XI Medici (A. Algardi, 1642-44); and the Stuart Monument (Canova, 1817-19). A door on the left aisle leads to the Treasury, containing early vestments, gold and silver, and ivories. There is a lift to the roof of the church, which commands a spectacular view. From the roof, steps lead to the lantern, allowing a close view of Michelangelo's dome. You can also descend to the Sacre Grotte Vaticane, containing the tombs of many popes. See **VATICAN, WALK 3.**

San Pietro in Vincoli: Begun in 431, this is one of the city's oldest churches, although it was considerably altered in later centuries. In a reliquary found under the high altar are preserved the chains which supposedly bound St. Peter during his periods of imprisonment in Rome and Jerusalem. The church's outstanding work of art is the tomb of Pope Julius II, designed by Michelangelo (see **A-Z**) and completed by his pupils. The magnificent figure of Moses was carved by the master himself and he may also have worked on the flanking figures of Leah and Rachel. See **CHURCHES 3, WALK 2.**

Sant'Agnese fuori le Mura: The 7thC church is built over the Catacombe di Sant'Agnese, the smallest of Rome's catacombs and dating from the 2nd-3rdC. This was the burial place of St. Agnes, a Christian martyr who died at the beginning of the 4thC. Her tomb is beneath the main altar and above it in the apse is a mosaic of the saint. Ask the warden for a tour of the catacombs and also for access to the nearby Mausoleo di Sant Costanza, built in the 4thC as the burial chapel of Costanza, daughter of Constantine (see **A-Z**), who built the first church of St. Agnes. The mausoleum was consecrated as a church in 1254. The central dome is carried by twelve double columns, and the tunnel-vaulted ambulatory is decorated with exquisite mosaics combining Christian and pagan subjects. See **CHURCHES 1**.

Santa Maria degli Angeli: Commissioned by Pope Pius IV in 1561, this basilica was Michelangelo's (see **A-Z**) last architectural work (when he was aged 86). The church design formed part of a larger scheme for the site of the Roman baths, the Terme di Diocleziano (see **A-Z**). The façade of the church is actually built into one of the surviving façades of the baths, while the main church is on the site of the *frigidarium* and the transept incorporates part of the *tepidarium*. Michelangelo's massive vaulting is entirely in keeping with the Roman architecture. In the transept is a solar meridian with signs of the zodiac designed by the astronomer Branchini in 1702. See **CHURCHES 1**.

Santa Maria del Popolo: This church contains some of the city's greatest works of art, many of them commissioned by Pope Sixtus IV and other members of the della Rovere family. The original 11thC foundation was rebuilt by Sixtus IV in 1474, and the interior was later remodelled by Bernini (see **A-Z**). The most notable paintings are those by Pintoricchio (see **A-Z**) in the della Rovere chapel (first on the right) and, above the high altar, two works by Caravaggio (see **A-Z**), the *Conversion of St. Paul* and the *Crucifixion of St. Peter*, in the first chapel of the left transept. There are also works by Annibale Caracci, Raphael (see **A-Z**), Sansovino, Bernini and Sebastiano del Piombo. See **CHURCHES 1**.

Santa Maria in Aracoeli: The Franciscans built this church in 1250 on the site of an 8thC monastery on the highest summit of the Campidoglio (see **A-Z**). Its name is taken from the altar (*ara coeli*) which, according to legend, was raised by Augustus (see **A-Z**) after he experienced a vision of the Madonna and Child here. The steep flight of 122 steps leading to the church from Piazza d'Aracoeli dates from 1348. The painting on the ceiling is the *Victory at Lepanto* (1571) by Marcantonio Colonna, and also notable are frescoes by Pintoricchio (see **A-Z**) depicting the *Life of St. Bernardino* and the *Santo Bambino* in the chapel of the Holy Child. See **CHURCHES 2, WALK 4**.

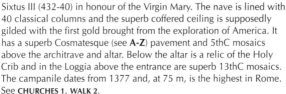

Santa Maria in Cosmedin: One of Rome's most attractive medieval churches, where worship follows the Byzantine or Eastern rite. Dating from the 6thC, it was altered in the 12thC. The seven-storey campanile, Cosmatesque (see **A-Z**) pavement, choir and portico date from this period. The portico contains the famous Bocca della Verità (see **A-Z**). See **CHURCHES 2, WALK 3.**

Santa Maria Maggiore: One of the four patriarchal basilicas, it sits on the summit of the Esquilino, and was built by Sixtus III (432-40) in honour of the Virgin Mary. The nave is lined with 40 classical columns and the superb coffered ceiling is supposedly gilded with the first gold brought from the exploration of America. It has a superb Cosmatesque (see **A-Z**) pavement and 5thC mosaics above the architrave and altar. Below the altar is a relic of the Holy Crib and in the Loggia above the entrance are superb 13thC mosaics. The campanile dates from 1377 and, at 75 m, is the highest in Rome. See **CHURCHES 1, WALK 2.**

Sistine Chapel: See Cappella Sistina.

Spanish Steps: See Piazza di Spagna.

Stanze di Raffaello: These are the four rooms of the Papal Apartments of the Vatican (see **VATICAN**) containing frescoes commissioned by Pope Julius II from Raphael (see **A-Z**). The first to be completed was the Stanza della Segnatura (1509-11), with paintings on the theme of human intellect. The *Disputà*, representing Christian theology, faces the much more famous *School of Athens*, often considered Raphael's greatest masterpiece, an ambitious composition showing the philosophers of ancient Greece. The blond figure at the lower left is a self-portrait. On one of the window walls is *Mount Parnassus*. Next to the Segnatura is the Stanza d'Eliodoro, painted between 1511 and 1514, and containing the *Expulsion of Heliodorus from the Temple*, the *Liberation of St. Peter* and the *Mass at Bolsena*. These are much more dramatic compositions whose richer colours may have been influenced by Michelangelo's (see **A-Z**) Sistine ceiling (see **Cappella Sistina**). The other two *stanze*, the Stanze dell'Incendio and the Sala di Constantino, contain some further dramatic paintings, notably the *Fire in the Borgo*, but were carried out by Raphael's pupils.

Teatro di Marcello: Begun by Julius Caesar (see **A-Z**) and completed by Augustus (see **A-Z**) in 13 BC for his nephew and son-in-law Marcellus. Due to its robust construction and strategic position overlooking the Tiber, it was converted into a fortress in the 12thC, partially incorporated into a *palazzo* in the 16thC and eventually passed into the possession of the Orsini family in 1712. Although only 12 of its original 41 arches in two tiers survive, it remains one of the city's most impressive monuments. See **ANCIENT ROME 2, WALKS 3 & 4**.

Terme di Caracalla: Ancient Rome's equivalent of today's public baths were in fact more than just baths. They actually comprised exercise rooms, a stadium, three large pools (cold, tepid and hot water), two libraries, an art gallery and a pleasure garden. The baths (completed by Emperor Caracalla in AD 216) could accommodate up to 1600 bathers. Little remains of the original, lavishly decorated interior. See **ANCIENT ROME 2**.

Terme di Diocleziano: Similar to the Terme di Caracalla (see **A-Z**) but even larger, they were built to serve the northern part of the city and completed by Emperor Diocletian in 305-06. The remains are now incorporated into a variety of buildings, including Santa Maria degli Angeli (see **A-Z**), designed by Michelangelo (see **A-Z**), and the Museo Nazionale Romano (see **A-Z**). See **ANCIENT ROME 2**.

Tivoli: The main attraction at this small town 35 km east of Rome is the Villa d'Este, with its famous gardens (0900-1 hr before sunset, Tue.-Sun.; fountains illuminated 2030-2330 April-Oct.; Expensive). A former Benedictine convent, it was redesigned by the Neapolitan architect Pirro Ligurio in 1550 for Cardinal Ippolito II d'Este, Governor of Tivoli. The old apartments covered with frescoes lead through to the beautiful terraced gardens filled with magnificent cascading fountains, including the Avenue of a Hundred Fountains, Oval Fountain, Organ Fountain, which used to emit a low musical note, Nature Fountain and Dragon Fountain. Buses from Rome leave from Via Gaeta, near Stazione Termini, or enquire at the tourist office for information on coach tours.

Trastevere: A lively and increasingly fashionable district 'across the Tiber' of narrow streets and small houses and squares. It was traditionally the home of artisans and dock workers, and the inhabitants claim to possess a more ancient and purer Roman ancestry than residents on the other side of the Tiber. In July the festival of Noiantri, 'we others', is held to celebrate this difference. See **WALK 3**.

Trevi Fountain: See **Fontana di Trevi**.

Trinità dei Monti: Dominating Piazza di Spagna (see **A-Z**) and the Spanish Steps, this church was founded by Louis XII of France in 1502 and completed in 1587. The Baroque façade is by Carlo Maderna, and inside in the Cappella Orsini is the fresco of *The Deposition* (c.1541) by Daniele de Volterra, which is regarded as his masterpiece. Piazza della Trinità dei Monti. M Spagna.

Vatican City: Città del Vaticano. Population c.1000. An independent sovereign state established by the Lateran Treaty of 1929 between the Holy See and Mussolini. Surrounded by walls except for San Pietro in Vaticano (see **A-Z**) and Piazza San Pietro, it covers 43 hectares. Legislative, executive and judicial authority resides with the Pope, who has his own bodyguard (Swiss Guard) who wear brightly-coloured medieval uniforms. The Vatican has its own bank, post office, newspaper, radio station, railway station and shops. Apart from the museums, St. Peter's and other specific areas, entry is forbidden without permission. See **VATICAN**.

Musei Vaticani

Via Appia Antica: The principal Roman consular road, built in 312 BC by Appius Claudius to link Rome with southeast Italy and, through the port of Brindisi, Greece, the Appian Way starts at Porta San Sebastiano (see **A-Z**). The tombs of rich Roman families are dotted along the road, as burials were not permitted within the city walls. Most of the tombs have been plundered by grave-robbers, or incorporated into later churches and other buildings. Apart from the catacombs (see **A-Z**), worth seeing are the little church of Domine Quo Vadis (supposedly on the site where St. Peter was met by a vision of Jesus and returned to the city and martyrdom) and the tomb of Cecilia Metella (1stC BC). See **ANCIENT ROME 3**.

Villa Adriana: Hadrian's Villa. This vast and sumptuous villa 28 km east of Rome was built by Emperor Hadrian (see **A-Z**) in AD 125-34 on his return from an extensive tour of the Roman Empire. He filled it with many art treasures he had collected during his trip, and some of the buildings clearly imitate the Greek and Egyptian styles. The visitor centre (0930-1.5 hr before sunset; Moderate) provides a helpful introduction. The site includes the colonnaded Picile based on the Stoa Poikile in Athens; the Philosophers' Hall; the Villa dell'Isola, where the emperor withdrew for quiet relaxation; and the Imperial Palace, some of whose floor mosaics survive. The most impressive structure is the Canopus, joined to the Serapeum buildings, modelled on a canal and temple of Serapis from the Nile Valley. Beside the Canopus is a small museum (0930-1 hr before sunset; Moderate) housing recent finds from the excavations. Buses from Rome leave from Via Gaeta, near Stazione Termini, or enquire at the tourist office for information on coach tours.

Villa Borghese: A large and splendid area of parkland created in the 17thC by Cardinal Scipione Borghese. There are woodlands, fountains, lakes, landscaped gardens, a small zoo (see **Children**) and the Pincio (see **A-Z**). See **MUSEUMS 1**.

Villa Farnesina: An elegant Renaissance villa built in 1510 by Peruzzi for the Sienese banker Chigi. See the superb fresco by Raphael (see **A-Z**) and the famous etchings by Piranesi in the Gabinetto delle Stampe. Via della Lungara 230. 0900-1300 Mon.-Sat. Bus 23, 65 from Piazza Venezia.

Villa Giulia: Built as a pleasant retreat for Pope Julius III in 1553, this building now houses the Museo Nazionale di Villa Giulia (see **MUSEUMS 2**), the most important collection of Etruscan art in the world. The many works of art displayed include a terracotta statue of Apollo and Hercules, and a beautiful sarcophagus with the smiling figures of a husband and wife reclining together. The villa itself is a Renaissance masterpiece, with a façade by Vignola, and many charming features by Bartolomeo Ammannati and Giorgio Vasari.

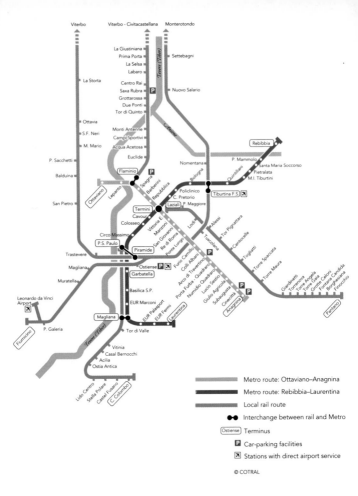

Viterbo
Viterbo - Civitacastellana
Monterotondo

La Giustiniana
Prima Porta
La Selsa
Labaro
Settebagni

Centro Rai
Saxa Rubra
Grottarossa
Due Ponti
Tor di Quinto
Nuovo Salario

La Storta

Ottavia
S.F. Neri
M. Mario
Monti Antenne
Campi Sportivi
Acqua Acetosa
Euclide

P. Sacchetti
Nomentana
Rebibbia
P. Mammolo
Santa Maria Soccorso
Pietralata
M.I. Tiburtini
Quintiliani

Balduina
Flaminio
Spagna
Barberini
Repubblica
Bologna

Ottaviano
Lepanto
Policlinico
C. Pretorio
P. Maggiore
Tiburtina F.S.

San Pietro
Termini
Laziali
Cavour
Vittoria E.
Manzoni
San Giovanni
Re di Roma
Ponte Lungo
Lodi
Alessi

Colosseo
Furio Camillo
Colli Albani
Tor Pignattara
Centocelle
Togliatti
Torre Spaccata

Circo Massimo
Arco di Travertino
Torre Maura

P.S. Paolo
Piramide
Porta Furba
Quadraro
Lucio Sestio
Giulio Agricola
Subaugusta
Cinecittà
Anagnina
Giardinetti
Torrenova
Torre Angela
Torre Gaia
Grotte Celoni
Fontana Candida
Borghesiana
Finocchio

Trastevere
Ostiense
Garbatella

Magliana
Muratella
Basilica S.P.

EUR Marconi
EUR Palasport
EUR Fermi

Leonardo da Vinci
Airport
Magliana
Tor di Valle
Laurentina
Pantano

Fiumicino
P. Galeria

Vitinia
Casal Bernocchi
Acilia
Ostia Antica

Lido Centro
Stella Polare
Castel Fusano
C. Colombo

	Metro route: Ottaviano–Anagnina
	Metro route: Rebibbia–Laurentina
	Local rail route
●●	Interchange between rail and Metro
Ostiense	Terminus
P	Car-parking facilities
✈	Stations with direct airport service

© COTRAL

Accidents & Breakdowns: In the event of an accident follow the usual procedure of exchanging names and addresses and insurance details. To contact the police or other emergency services, tel: 113. If someone is injured and you are held responsible, insist on contacting your consulate (see **A-Z**) as soon as possible. If you break down, a red warning triangle should be placed 50 m behind your vehicle. Tel: 116 for the ACI (Automobile Club d'Italia). There are emergency telephones at 1 km intervals along motorways. Press the red button for medical assistance and the green button for the breakdown service. See **Driving**.

Accommodation: There are countless hotels and *pensioni* (guest-houses) in Rome. Hotels are rated from de luxe and 1st to 4th class and *pensioni* from P1 to P3. Prices (1993) range from about L.80,000 for a double room with a bath in the cheapest categories to L.150,000 for mid-priced hotels and *pensioni*, to L.500,000 or more in de luxe hotels. By law, prices are displayed on the door of the room, and are usually exclusive of breakfast, but should include services and taxes. The peak season is April-Oct. but demand is high all year, especially for medium-priced establishments in the historic centre around the Pantheon, Piazza Navona and Piazza Campo dei Fiori, so booking is essential to ensure good quality and a decent area. There are many cheap establishments around Stazione Termini but the area is rather drab. Luxury accommodation is concentrated around Via Vittorio Veneto, Villa Borghese, Spagna and Barberini. The EPT (see **Tourist Information**) provides accommodation advice and a list of hotels. Its offices at Stazione Termini, Fiumicino (see **Airports**) and at the main motorway entrances to the city also have a free booking service. See **Camping & Caravanning**, **Youth Hostels**.

Airports: Leonardo da Vinci (Fiumicino), 36 km southwest of Rome, handles the bulk of international and domestic flights, tel: 65954455/3640. Facilities include toilets, restaurants, bars, accommodation, shops, car hire, etc. There are regular train services to Rome's Ostiense (M Piramide) and Tiburtina (M Tiburtina) stations. Taxis are quicker but a lot more expensive.

Ciampino airport, 16 km south on Via Appia Nuova, handles mainly charter flights, tel: 794941. It has all the usual facilities and there is a regular bus service to Stazione Termini.

Archaeological Sites: A number of the sites of ancient Rome can be viewed from outside but are not open for visits by the general public due to work in progress or the fragile condition of the remains. Visitors with a serious interest in Roman archaeology may contact Ripartizione, Via del Portico d'Ottavia 29, tel: 67103819, about access to the Circo Massimo (see **A-Z**), Fori Imperiali (see **A-Z**) and other sites. See **ANCIENT ROME 1-3**.

Baby-sitters: Ask at your hotel or *pensione* for details of baby-sitting services, or consult the telephone directory. See **Children**.

Banks: See **Currency, Money, Opening Times**.

Best Buys: The superb quality of Italian design is recognized worldwide, and shopping in Rome is a treat – if you can afford it. Leather goods, especially handbags and shoes, are recommended, and Rome is also an important centre for fashion, jewellery and antiques. But it must be emphasized that there are few bargains. See **SHOPPING 1-3**, **Markets, Shopping**.

Bicycle & Motorcycle Hire: Cycling is not recommended in the centre of Rome, given the sheer volume of traffic and aggressive tactics of Roman drivers. However, a bicycle ride round Villa Borghese is extremely pleasant. Bicycles can be hired from ACI Parking, Piazza del Popolo, tel: 311923, or Collati, Via del Pellegrino 82, tel: 6541084/ 6881084. Motorcycles and scooters are more practical, but should only be considered by those with experience and nerves of steel. Hiring outlets are Motonoleggio, Via della Purificazione 66 (off Piazza Barberini), tel: 465485, and Scoot-a-Long, Via Cavour 302, tel: 6780206.

Budget: 1993 prices.

Hotel breakfast	L.10,000-15,000
Lunch/dinner main course	L.10,000-30,000
Tourist menu	L.20,000-30,000
Ice cream (takeaway)	L.2000-3000 per scoop
(sitting)	L.9000-14,000
Bus ticket	from L.1200
Coffee	L.1500-7000
Bottle of wine with meal	L.13,000-30,000

Buses: Buses are the main form of transport in Rome. The ATAC network of orange buses covers the whole city. The main terminal and information office is in Piazza dei Cinquecento, outside Stazione Termini. Tickets must be bought in advance at booths at the bus terminal or at tobacconists, bars and newspaper kiosks, and have to be stamped in a machine on boarding. Each standard ticket is valid for two journeys made within 1.5 hr and is also valid on trams (see **A-Z**). One-day tickets, called BIG, and weekly tourist tickets for unlimited travel on buses, trams and the Metro (see **A-Z**) are available from the ATAC information office. Although many of the locals do not bother to stamp their tickets (if they have them) beware: there are inspectors and fines are high. One of the most useful buses is No. 64 to St. Peter's, which passes many of the most important tourist sights. Night buses, *servizio notturno*, run from 2400. Schedules and routes are posted at bus stops, and you can buy a useful bus map of the city, detailing all services, from the ATAC office and from newsagents.

Esposizione Universale Romana

Cameras & Photography: Tripods and flashes are forbidden in museums and some churches. Film and photographic and video equipment are widely available but expensive. Outlets are: Tonel, Via di Porta Cavalleggeri 15-19, tel: 632896; Fotoottica Pandimiglio, Via Flaminia 41a, tel: 3203544. A fast processing service (1 hr or less) is available at Cine Photo Service, Via del Trullo 114, tel: 6539809; D&B, Lungotevere dei Mellini 38, tel: 3220972; Foto Smack, Via Baldassarre Castiglione 72-76, tel: 5414368.

Camping & Caravanning: The nearest camp sites to the city are on the main approach roads: Roma, Via Aurelia 831, tel: 6623018/6628863/66418147; Flaminio, Via Flaminia (8.2 km), tel: 3330653/3332516/3332604; Seven Hills, Via Cassia 1216, tel: 3765100/30310214/30310826; Capitol, Ostica Antica, Via Castelfusano 45, tel: 5662720.

Car Hire: You need a valid driving licence which you should have held for at least one year and you must be over 21 years of age. Unless you are paying by credit card you will have to leave a deposit. The main companies (Avis, Budget, Hertz, etc.) have desks at Fiumicino and Ciampino (see **Airports**) and Stazione Termini. Your hotel may have leaflets on local companies which are often cheaper, but remember to check details of insurance and mileage. See **Driving**.

Chemists: Chemists have the same opening times (see **A-Z**) as shops. Late-night chemists: Galleria di Testa, Termini; Piram, Via Nazionale 228. Tel: 192 for addresses of chemists open outside normal hours, or check the notices displayed by all chemists. See **Health**.

Children: A large, busy city like Rome is not an ideal place for children, but there is a variety of attractions which should help keep them amused. Besides a trip to the Foro Romano (see **A-Z**) or the Colosseo (see **A-Z**), which should excite the imagination, there are beautiful parks such as Villa Borghese (see **A-Z**), Villa Ada and Villa Glori, which have playgrounds, pony-riding, roller-skating, etc. Villa Borghese also has a small zoo, the Giardino Zoologico (0830-sunset; Moderate. Flaminio). Luna Park in EUR (see **A-Z**) is the largest amusement park in Italy and offers plenty of thrills (Via delle Tre Fontane, EUR, 1600-2400 Mon.-Sat., 1000-2400 Sun.; Expensive. EUR Fermi). The Museo delle Cere is a wax museum displaying famous figures from Italian history (Piazza Venezia 67, 0900-2000; Inexpensive. Bus 64 to Piazza Venezia). Piazza Navona (see **A-Z**), a traffic-free area with small street stalls selling toys and balloons, is also a popular spot with children. Check newspapers (see **What's On**) for any special events for children. See **Baby-sitters**.

Climate: Spring is usually dry and sunny, with temperatures ranging from 18°C to 28°C. Summers are hot, sometimes unbearably so, with temperatures soaring to 35°C-40°C at midday in July and Aug. Autumn is the best time to visit the city (Oct. is perfect) – it is still warm, but not too hot for sightseeing, and less crowded. Winters are mild, and, although there is the odd frozen spell in Jan. and Feb., snow is rare.

Complaints: Ask to see the manager or owner of the premises if you find you have been overcharged or the price on the bill does not correspond to that displayed in the room. If you are still not satisfied, contact the EPT (see **Tourist Information**) or the police (see **A-Z**). However, the threat of such action is usually sufficient to get results.

Consulates:

UK – Via XX Settembre 80a, tel: 4825441.
Republic of Ireland – Largo Nazzareno 3, tel: 6782541.
Australia – Via Alessandria 215, tel: 832721/852721.
Canada – Via Zara 30, tel: 4403028.
New Zealand – Via Zara 28, tel: 4402928.
USA – Via Vittorio Veneto 121, tel: 46741.

Conversion Chart:

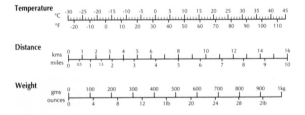

Credit Cards: See **Money**.

Crime & Theft: The large number of tourists and pilgrims who visit Rome each year does unfortunately mean that some of them are the targets of crime, usually theft in the street or on public transport. Keep all valuables and large amounts of cash in the hotel safe. Carry your wallet in a secure pocket and keep your handbag under your arm or wear it across your body. Never leave baggage unattended or visible in a locked car. Keep the serial numbers of your traveller's cheques separately, along with a note of your passport number; if they are lost or stolen notify the office where they were issued immediately. If you lose your passport notify the police (see **A-Z**) and your consulate (see **A-Z**). Carry car documents with you to prove ownership in case of theft. Keep a copy of police reports for insurance claims. See **Emergency Numbers**.

Currency: The lira (plural lire) is the Italian monetary unit, shown as L. or, confusingly, £, before the figure.
Coins – 10, 20, 50, 100, 200, 500 lire.
Notes – 1000, 2000, 5000, 10,000, 50,000, 100,000 lire.
Coins are very scarce and change is often given in the form of *gettoni* (telephone tokens). See **Money**.

Customs Allowances:

UK/EC	Cigarettes	Cigarillos	Cigars	Tobacco	Still Table Wine	Spirits/Liqueurs	Fortified Wine	Additional Still Table Wine	Perfume	Toilet Water	Gifts & Souvenirs
Duty Free	200 *or*	100 *or*	50 *or*	250 g	2 *l*	1 *l* *or*	2 *l* *or*	2 *l*	60 cc/ml	250 cc/ml	£32
Duty Paid	800	400	200	1 kg	90 *l**	10 *l*	20 *l*				

* Of which no more than 60 l should be sparkling wine

With the Single European Market, travellers are subject only to highly selective spot checks. The red and green channels no longer apply within the EC. There is no restriction, either by quantity or value, on *duty-paid* goods purchased in another country, provided they are for the purchaser's *own personal use* (guidelines have been published). If you are unsure of certain items, check with the customs officials as to whether payment of duty is required.

Disabled People: As in many cities, provision of access and special facilities for wheelchair users is still rather patchy in Rome. Public transport, for example, is not yet wheelchair-friendly. There are wheelchair-access toilets at Fiumicino and Ciampino airports, at Stazione Termini, near platfom 1, and at Piazza San Pietro. St. Peter's and the Vatican Museums are well equipped, with lifts and wheelchair routes clearly signposted. Many of the other major museums and galleries also now have wheelchair access (including toilets). A list of Rome's museums published by the EPT (see **Tourist Information**) gives the wheelchair access sign where applicable. Around the most popular tourist areas many permanent kerbs have ramps. Mention any special needs when making hotel or restaurant reservations. For more details, contact the EPT. See **Health**, **Insurance**.

Drinks: Ask for the house wine (*il vino della casa*) in cheaper restaurants, as this is usually good value. Most establishments offer a varied selection of wines, including local favourites such as Frascati and Marino, and national varieties such as Chianti and Orvieto. Carbonated mineral water (*acqua minerale gasata*) is very popular, and there is usually a selection of beers (*birra*) and fruit juices. Coffee (*un caffè*) is espresso, small and strong; for coffee with milk order a *caffellatte*; an espresso with just a drop of milk is called *macchiato*; cappuccino is made with frothy milk sprinkled with chocolate. Tea is also widely available, with milk or lemon (*al limone*). Grappa is a strong grape-skin liqueur made in the north of Italy, and is popular after meals.

Driving: Driving in Rome can be a nerve-racking and frustrating experience due to severe congestion, a confusing one-way system, the closure to traffic of many central streets, and severe competition for the limited number of parking spaces available. If you do venture onto the roads, remember to drive on the right, and give way to traffic coming from the right – although these rules are not always followed! The speed limit in built-up areas is nominally 50 kph; on motorways 130 kph Mon.-Fri., 110 kph Sat. and Sun. Third-party insurance is obligatory if you bring your own car, and make sure you have your driving licence, car registration papers and a national identity sticker. You must also carry a red warning triangle in case of breakdowns (see **Accidents**

& Breakdowns). Petrol coupons (giving discounts on petrol) and motorway vouchers (for use at motorway tolls) are available for foreign motorists bringing their own cars (though not if you hire a car). These are available from motoring organizations at home or Automobile Club Italiano (ACI) branches at border crossings (not within Italy). See **Parking**, **Petrol**.

Drugs: All drugs are illegal and there are severe penalties for offenders. Contact your consulate (see **A-Z**) if you are arrested for a drugs-related offence.

Eating Out: There are literally thousands of eating places in Rome, ranging from élite establishments to simple trattorias serving cheap, local dishes. Pizzerias, *rosticcerie* (which serve hot food and take-aways), self-service and fast-food outlets are also widespread. Italians demand high standards of cooking, so that even the most humble-looking establishments are likely to prove more than acceptable. The restaurant at Stazione Termini, for example, serves delicious food. Most tourists won't be able to afford a lavish meal every day for lunch and dinner, so try asking for the tourist menu (*menu turistico*) which normally costs L.20,000-30,000 for a two- or three-course meal. A service charge of around 15% is normally added to all bills and most restaurants also have a cover charge (*coperto*). See CAFÉS, RESTAURANTS 1-3, **Food**.

Electricity: 220 V. Two-pin plugs are used and adaptors are widely available in Italy and in the UK.

Emergency Numbers:

Police, fire and ambulance	113
Ambulance and Red Cross	5100
Carabinieri	112 or 85291
City police	67691
Fire brigade	115 or 46721
ACI breakdown service	116 or 5106

Events:

January: Befana, toys and sweets fair on Piazza Navona (ends 6 Jan.)

February: Carnival and Lenten celebrations, young children dress up and shower the streets with water and flour bombs.

19 March: Feast of St. Joseph celebrated in the Trionfale district, where traditional hot fritters are served from stalls in the streets.

April: Holy Week, religious services celebrated in all of Rome's churches. *Good Fri.:* The Pope takes part in the stations of the Cross procession from the Colosseo to the Palatino. *Easter Day:* At 1200 the Pope gives the blessing *urbi et orbi* from the loggia of St. Peter's; *21:* Celebration of the founding of Rome in Piazza del Campidoglio; *late April:* Azalea Show in Piazza di Spagna, the most beautiful azalea blooms from the city's nurseries are displayed on the Spanish Steps.

May: Antique Fair in Via dei Coronari; *1-15 June:* Rose Show in Valle Murcia rosery on the Aventino; *8-11:* Art Exhibition in Via Margutta.

June: International Trade Fair (Fiera di Roma), Via Cristoforo Colombo; *24:* Feast of St. John the Baptist, various events take place in the San Giovanni district, and traditionally large quantities of snails are consumed.

June-Sep.: Estate Musica and Estate Romana, cultural entertainments organized by the Rome EPT (see **Tourist Information**) and municipality.

July: Feast of Noiantri, the people of Trastevere hold folk concerts and sports contests in honour of their ancestors.

August: Festa della Madonna della Neve, in Santa Maria Maggiore; *1:* Feste delle Catene, in the church of San Pietro in Vincoli.

September: Children's Expo at the Fiera di Roma; National Antique Fair at the Fiera di Roma.

October: Art Fair in Via Margutta; Handicraft Trade Fair in Via dell'Orso.

November: Rome Motor Show at the Fiera di Roma.

December: Beautiful Nativity scenes are displayed in many churches throughout the city; Festa della Madonna Immacolata, in Piazza di Spagna; *31:* Solemn Te Deum in the church of Il Gesù.

For further details, pick up a copy of *Un Anno a Roma e provincia*, a booklet published by the EPT and available at its offices.

Food: Roman meals usually start with *antipasti*, and you are often able to serve yourself from a delicious selection of cooked and raw vegetables, seafood, omelettes and salads. Traditionally this is followed by a pasta course. Typical Roman offerings are: *spaghetti alla carbonara* (bacon, garlic and beaten egg); *penne all'arrabbiata* (pasta tubes with a spicy tomato sauce); *spaghetti all'amatriciana* (tomato sauce with salt pork or ham); and gnocchi (potato dumplings in a sauce). Popular main courses include: *saltimbocca* (veal fillet with ham and sage cooked in white wine); *ossobuco* (stewed veal knuckles); *abbacchio* (roast lamb); *pollo alla cacciatore* (chicken with tomato and herb sauce); and *trippa* (tripe). The meal is usually completed with cheeses such as pecorino (made from ewe's milk) or fresh mozzarella, fruit, or *gelato* (ice cream), an Italian speciality which comes in many exotic flavours. See CAFÉS, RESTAURANTS 1-3, **Eating Out**.

Health: Before leaving the UK you should obtain form E111 from the DSS, which entitles you to free medical treatment while you are in Italy. Present the form to any (State) doctor you consult, who will then arrange for you to be exempted from payment. You should also take out private insurance to cover the costs of repatriation in case of serious illness. The principal hospitals are:

Policlinico Umberto I, Viale del Policlinico, tel: 4469909.
San Camillo Hospital, Circonvallazione Gianicolense 87, tel: 58701.
San Giovanni Hospital, Via dell'Amba Aradam 8, tel: 77051.
Santo Spirito Hospital, Lungotevere in Sassia 1, tel: 6838901.
G. Eastman Dental Hospital, Viale Regina Elena 287b, tel: 4457206/ 4469844.
For urgent blood transfusions, tel: 4456375/7705563.
See **Chemists**, **Insurance**.

Piazza Campo dei Fiori

Insurance: You should take out travel insurance to cover you against theft and loss of property and money, as well as medical expenses, for the duration of your stay. Your travel agent should be able to recommend a suitable policy. See **Crime & Theft**, **Driving**, **Health**.

Laundries: Ask at your hotel or *pensione*. Launderettes in Rome are not self-service: you leave your washing and will be told when to collect it. The price depends on the weight of clothes. In the city centre try Scerna, Largo Magna Grecia 22, or Zampa, Piazza Campo dei Fiori 38.

Lost Property: Report any loss or theft to the police (see **A-Z**) immediately. There are lost property offices at all airports and railway termini. The municipal transport office (ATAC) is at Via Volturno 65, near Stazione Termini (1000-1200), and the municipal lost property office at Via Nicolo Bettoni 1 (0900-1200).

Markets: Rome's most lively market is the Sun. morning flea market at Porta Portese in Trastevere, but watch out for pickpockets (streets off Trastevere; Bus 56, 60, 75, 170). Other markets can be found in Piazza Campo dei Fiori (fresh produce and second-hand clothes; 0600-1400

Mon.-Sat. Bus 26, 62, 64, 90); Piazza Vittorio Emanuele II (general market; 0700-1400 Mon.-Sat. M Termini); Via Trionfale and Via Paolo Sarpi (flowers; 1000-1300 Tue. M Ottaviano then Bus 70); and Via Sannino (second-hand clothes and accessories; 0800-1300 Mon.-Fri., 0800-1900 Sat. M San Giovanni). See **Shopping**.

Metro: The Rome underground, the Metro or Metropolitana, has only two lines, A and B, which cross at Stazione Termini. M Tiburtina and M Piramide (Stazione Ostiense) have connections with trains to Leonardo da Vinci (Fiumicino) airport. Standard tickets are for one journey only and can be purchased at ticket offices and machines in Metro stations. Note that some stations only have ticket machines. If you intend using public transport a lot, it's cheaper to buy one-day or weekly tickets for the whole public transport network (see **Buses**).

Money: Foreign currency and traveller's cheques can be changed in banks, bureaux de change (*cambio*) and larger hotels on the production of a passport. Major credit cards are widely accepted and many shops and hotels also accept payment by traveller's cheques or in foreign currency, but often charge a high commission (check the rate they offer first). There are exchange bureaux at: Stazione Termini; Piazza di Spagna 38 (American Express); Aurum, Via della Vite 18; Cambio Roma, Via F. Crispi 15; Società Rosati, Via Nazionale 186; Via Viaggi, Via dei Due Macelli 109; and Eurocambio, Via F. Crispi 92. See **Currency**, **Opening Times**.

Museums & Art Galleries: Rome has a large number of museums and galleries, many of them small and devoted to special subjects. Apart from the major museums and galleries listed in the topics section of this guide, the following may be of interest:
Museo Nazionale delle Arte e Tradizioni Popolari, Piazza Guglielmo Marconi 8, EUR. 0900-1400 Mon.-Sat., 0900-1300 Sun.; Inexpensive. Museum of popular arts and traditions.
Galleria Nazionale di Palazzo Corsini, Via della Lungara 10. 0900-1400 Tue.-Sat., 0900-1300 Sun.; Moderate. Collection of 16th and 17thC art.

Museo di Roma, Palazzo Braschi, Piazza San Pantaleo 10 (temporarily closed in 1993). Interpretative displays of Roman life in the 16th-19thC. See WALK 4.

Galleria Comunale d'Arte Moderna, Palazzo Braschi, Piazza San Pantaleo 10 (temporarily closed in 1993). Collection of 19thC art, including watercolours by Bartolomeo Pinelli. See WALK 4.

Museo della Civiltà Romana, Piazza Giovanni Agnelli, EUR. 0900-1330 Tue.-Sat. (also 1500-1800 Tue. & Thu.), 0900-1300 Sun.; Inexpensive.

Museo di Arte Ebraica, Lungotevere dei Cenci. 0930-1400, 1500-1700 Mon.-Thu., 0930-1400 Fri., 0930-1230 Sun.; Inexpensive. Museum of the Jewish community in Rome.

Museo degli Strumenti Musicali, Piazza di Santa Croce in Gerusalemme 9a. 0900-1330 Mon.-Sat.; Inexpensive. More than 800 musical instruments on display.

Museo Nazionale delle Paste Alimentari, Piazza Scanderberg. 0930-1230 Mon.-Sat.; Inexpensive. Rome's newest museum, devoted to the history of pasta-making.

See MUSEUMS 1 & 2, VATICAN.

Music: Opera and ballet are performed (Dec.-June) at the Teatro dell'Opera, Piazza Beniamino Gigli 1. Tickets are available 48 hr before the performance begins (box office 1000-1300, 1700-1900 Tue.-Sat.). During July and Aug. the theatre moves to the Terme di Caracalla, where tickets are on sale on the day of the performance. Orchestral concerts by the famous Accademia di Santa Cecilia are held in the Auditorio di Via della Conciliazione, Via della Conciliazione 4, and the Accademia Filarmonica performs in the Teatro Olimpico, Piazza Gentile da Fabriano 17. Famous basilicas hold one-off performances of recitals and choral concerts, and there are music festivals in the parks during the summer. There are also live music venues, including jazz and rock clubs (see NIGHTLIFE, **Nightlife**). A booklet published every year by the EPT (see **Tourist Information**), *Un Anno in Roma e provincia*, gives details of opera, concert and theatre seasons and special festivals. Details of cultural events are also given in the newspapers (see **What's On**).

Newspapers: Foreign newspapers and magazines are widely available in kiosks and newsagents all over the city. See **What's On**.

Nightlife: There is a variety of bars, nightclubs, discos and music venues to suit all tastes. Productions of de Filippo, Goldoni, Pirandello and other classics are generally given by the Eliseo, Via Nazionale 183, Parioli, Via Borsi 20, and Argentina, Largo di Torre Argentina. The Sistina, Via Sistina 129-30, features musicals and international variety acts. Box offices usually open 1000-1300, 1600-1900, but times do vary. For movie-goers, the Pasquino, Vicolo del Piede 19a, off Piazza di Santa Maria in Trastevere, is one of the few cinemas which show English-language films in the original (usually two or three showings, starting at 1600). See NIGHTLIFE, **Music**.

Opening Times: These can vary enormously, but in general:
Banks – 0830-1330, 1500-1600 Mon.-Fri.
Retail shops – 0900-1300, 1600-1930. Closed Mon. am and Sun.
Supermarkets and food shops – 0800-1330, 1700-1930. Closed Sat. pm in summer and Thu. pm in winter.
Churches – 0700-1200, 1600-1900.
Museums – 0900/1000-1300/1400, 1400/1500-1700/1800 (1300 Sun. & hols) Tue.-Sun. Note that last admission is 30 min to 1 hr before museums close.
Post offices – 0800-1400 Mon.-Sat.

Parking: Parking in Rome is a nightmare. Cars far outnumber parking places, and double and triple parking is normal. There are official car parks on all the main routes into the city centre, and the largest city car park is under the Villa Borghese. Illegally parked cars are towed away by the traffic police. Should this happen to you, contact the Commando dei Vigili Urbani, Via della Conciliazione 4, tel: 676938. See **Driving**.

Passports & Customs: A valid passport (or identity card for some EC visitors) is necessary, but no visa is required for stays of less than three months. There is no limit on the amount of money you can bring in or out of the country, but amounts over a million lire must be declared on the V2 form on entry. See **Customs Allowances**.

Petrol: There are petrol stations at frequent intervals along all the major routes into and out of the city (0700-1230, 1500-1900 Oct.-April, 0700-1230, 1530-1930 May-Sep.). Central petrol stations with extended opening hours are: Appio Tuscolano (Total), Via Appia Nuova/Via dei Cessati Spiriti; Flaminio (Mobil), Corso di Francia/Via Vigna Stelluti; Trastevere (Agip), Lungotevere Ripa 8. See **Driving**.

Police: There are several types of police in the city: the Carabinieri, tel: 212121, who deal with serious crimes; the Policia, tel: 67691, who deal with general crime and administrative problems, including lost passports and theft reports for insurance claims; and the Vigili Urbani and Polizia Stradale, who deal with traffic problems inside and outside the city respectively. See **Crime & Theft**, **Emergency Numbers**.

Post Offices: The head post office, in Piazza di San Silvestro, has a 24 hr telegram and international phone service (telex/fax), and poste restante facilities (0830-2100 Mon.-Fri., 0800-1200 Sat.). Stamps are sold at tobacconists (displaying a 'T' sign) and hotels as well as post offices. Vatican City has its own stamps and postmarks, and its own post office in Piazza San Pietro. Postcards, etc. must be posted in the special blue postboxes in the piazza or souvenir shops near the Vatican. See **Opening Times**, **Telephones & Telegrams**.

Public Holidays: 1 Jan.; Easter Mon.; 25 April (Liberation Day); 1 May (Labour Day); 15 Aug. (Assumption); 1 Nov. (All Saints' Day); 8 Dec. (Immaculate Conception); 25 Dec.; 26 Dec.

Rabies: Still a danger here as in other parts of the Continent. As a precaution, have all animal bites examined immediately by a doctor.

Railways: Rome's main railway station is Stazione Termini, with direct services to continental destinations and all the main Italian cities, including Florence, Milan, Naples and Genoa. Services are reliable and reasonably priced (enquire about discounts). Tel: 4775 or contact the EPT (see **Tourist Information**) for information. The fastest trains are the Trans-Europe Express (TEE) and the Intercity (IC), which stop at major destinations only (reserve in advance). The Rapido (R) and Espresso (ES) are also express services and only stop at large towns. The Diretto (D), Locale (L), Accelerato (A) and Littorina (L) are all fairly slow local services which stop frequently.

Religious Services: Roman Catholic – Mass is celebrated up to 1300 and 1700-2000 Sun. (and often weekdays) in main churches. High Mass is celebrated in the seven basilicas on Sun. at 0930/1000. Roman Catholic services in English are held in San Silvestro in Capite, St. Thomas of Canterbury and Santa Susanna. Confessions are heard in English in the four main basilicas.
Anglican – All Saints, Via del Babuino 153b.
American Episcopal – St. Paul's, Via Nazionale.
Methodist – Ponte Sant'Angelo, Via del Banco di Santo Spirito 3.
Jewish – Lungotevere dei Cenci.

Shopping: The best (and most expensive) shops are situated in the streets around Piazza di Spagna. These include top outlets for fashion wear, shoes, jewellery, furs, leather garments and accessories. Via dei Corarari is famous for its antique shops selling furniture, silver, jewellery, pictures, etc., and a similar selection can be found along Via del Babuino. There is also a small shopping area near the Pantheon which is less expensive. Most shops will happily arrange to post purchases abroad. See **SHOPPING 1-3**, **Best Buys**, **Markets**, **Opening Times**.

Smoking: Not permitted on public transport or in the auditoriums of theatres and cinemas. However, smoking is still widely tolerated.

Sports: The Foro Italico sports complex (1931), north of Monte Mario, contains the Stadio Olimpico, where football teams from Rome and Lazio play every other Sun. afternoon, Sep.-May. The stadium can hold crowds of up to 100,000. There are also open-air and enclosed swimming pools, lawn tennis and basketball courts, running tracks and many other facilities. Another sports centre, the Tre Fontane at EUR, contains the Piscina delle Rose, a 50 m open-air swimming pool (Viale America; 0900-1230, 1400-1900 June-Sep. M EUR Marconi). There is horse racing at Tor di Valle, 9 km southwest of Via del Mare, and an international horse show is held in the Villa Borghese April-May.

Taxis: Taxis are yellow and must be hired from ranks or summoned by telephone: Radio Taxi Roma, tel: 3570; Radio Taxi La Capitale, tel: 4994. There are supplements for extra luggage, for night service (2200-0700), and on Sun. and hols. A small tip is expected.

Telephones & Telegrams: You will find public telephones on many streets, in railway stations, in bars and newsagents (displaying the yellow sign), and at the Centro Telefonico Pubblico (SIP) in Stazione Termini and Piazza di San Silvestro. Newer coin-operated phones take L.100, L.200 and L.500 coins. Other phones use phone cards worth L.1000 and L.5000, which can be purchased at tobacconists, but some of the older ones still only accept *gettoni* (telephone tokens), which can be purchased in bars, hotels, newsagents, tobacconists and post offices for L.200. It is best to make international calls from the main post office or SIP kiosks. To direct dial abroad, first dial 00 followed by the country code (UK – 44, USA – 1), then remember to omit the first zero of the city code before dialling the rest of the number. There is a 24 hr telegram service at the head post office (see **A-Z**), or you can send one by phone, tel: 186. A cheaper, more efficient, alternative is a night letter/telegram which is guaranteed to arrive the next morning. See **Emergency Numbers**.

Television & Radio: Italy has three state-owned television channels run by RAI, and three privately-owned national channels: Rotequattro, Canale 5 and Italia 1. In addition, there are a vast number of private local channels. RAI channels show a high proportion of music and arts programmes. Most hotels also have cable or satellite TV with English-speaking channels. On the radio, the BBC World Service can usually be picked up and there is a wide choice of RAI and independent Italian channels.

Time Difference: Rome is 1 hr ahead of GMT in winter and 2 hr ahead of GMT in summer.

Tipping: Although restaurant, café and hotel bills usually include a service charge, it is customary to leave a 10% tip if you are happy with the service. Taxi drivers, cinema and theatre ushers, hairdressers, toilet attendants and guides also expect to be tipped. Porters should be given L.1000 per item.

Toilets: Public toilets are unfortunately in short supply in Rome. Most people pop into cafés or bars and, if necessary, have a drink before using the facilities. There are public toilets at Stazione Termini, at Fiumicino and Ciampino airports, and at the major galleries and muse-ums. In the Metro station at Stazione Termini there is also an *albergo diurno*, a 'day hotel', with toilets, washing facilities and showers (0640-2040 daily).

Tourist Information: The Ente Nazionale il Turismo (ENIT) office, Via Maghera 2, tel: 4971222/82, will help you with any queries and advise you on such matters as accommodation. It also provides free maps. The regional office, Ente Provinciale per il Turismo (EPT), for Rome is at Via Parigi 11, tel: 461851 (0820-1340 Mon.-Fri., 0820-1330 Sat.), and there are branches at Stazione Termini, Fiumicino airport arrivals hall, and at motorway service areas at Saleria Ovest (on the A1 from Milan and Florence) and Frascati Est (on the A2 from Naples).

Tours: Various travel agencies run tours of the city and to the Castelli Romani (see **EXCURSION 1**), Cerveteri, Tivoli (see **A-Z**), Bracciano (see **EXCURSION 2**) and other places. Carrani Tours, Via Vittorio Emanuele Orlando 95, tel: 4742501, runs coach tours in the city and environs

Villa d'Este, Tivoli

with multilingual guides. Walk History, tel: 4750731/0774-8387666 arranges guided walking tours of the city. Tour Visa, tel: 493481, runs boat trips along the Tiber (April-Sep.) and to Ostia Antica (see **A-Z**). ATAC runs bus tours of the city from the terminus outside the station (Bus 110). Guided tours of the Vatican (see **A-Z**) are also available. Contact the EPT (see **Tourist Information**) for more details.

Trams: There are only six tram services left in Rome, the rest having been replaced by buses. A ride on Tram 30 is a useful way of getting one's bearings, as its route is a circuit of much of the city. Trams have the same tickets as buses (see **A-Z**).

Transport: The best way of getting round the city, apart from walking, is by local bus. In summer you can hire a horse-drawn carriage (*carrozzella*) in Piazza di Spagna or outside the Colosseo; establish the fare before you set off. To explore the towns and countryside around Rome you may wish to hire a car or book a coach excursion (see **Tours**). There are also reliable bus and train services to destinations throughout the region. The best means of intercity travel is the train, which is fast, reliable and good value. See **Airports**, **Buses**, **Metro**, **Railways**, **Taxis**, **Trams**.

Colosseo

Traveller's Cheques: See **Money**.

What's On: For information on events in Rome, check the listings in the following publications: *La Settimana a Roma* (available in English as *This Week in Rome*); the Fri. *Il Messaggero*; and *Trovaroma* in the Thu. *La Repubblica*. Listings are also published in *Wanted in Rome*, a free English-language newsletter which appears every two weeks and is distributed to bars, restaurants and newsagents. *Carnet di Roma* is a free monthly bulletin for tourists available from the EPT (see **Tourist Information**), which has listings and articles on upcoming attractions. See **Events**.

Youth Hostels: The only hostel in Rome is the Ostello per la Gioventù Foro Italico, Viale delle Olimpiadi 61, tel: 3236267/3236279 (350 beds). There is also the YWCA, Via Cesare Balbo 4, and the Salvation Army, Via degli Apuli 39-41. For more details of cheap accommodation, contact the EPT (see **Tourist Information**).

This edition published 1995 by Diamond Books
77–85 Fulham Palace Road
Hammersmith, London W6 8JB

Text: Callum Brines with additional
information by Hilary Macartney
Photography: Michael Dent & Keith Allardyce
Electronic Cartography: Susan Harvey Design
and Iain Robinson (1, 56)

First published 1990 Second edition 1994
Copyright © HarperCollins *Publishers*

Printed in Italy

ISBN 0 261 66596-0

Foro Romano